A SYNOD DIARY

A SYNOD DIARY

Sixty Days That Shook the Church

Michael W. Higgins

Paulist Press
New York / Mahwah, NJ

NOVALIS

Library of Congress Cataloging-in-Publication Data
Names: Higgins, Michael W., 1948– author
Title: A Synod diary: sixty days that shook the Church / Michael W. Higgins.
Description: New York: [Paulist Press], [2026] | Includes bibliographical references. | Summary: "Eyewitness account of the events surrounding the Synod on Synodality, held at the Vatican in 2023 and 2024"—Provided by publisher.
Identifiers: LCCN 2025016696 (print) | LCCN 2025016697 (ebook) | ISBN 9780809157112 paperback | ISBN 9780809188666 ebook
Subjects: LCSH: Catholic Church. Synod Extraordinary (1985: Rome, Italy) | Catholic Church. Synodus Episcoporum | Catholic Church—History—1965–
Classification: LCC BX837.5 .H54 2026 (print) | LCC BX837.5 (ebook)
LC record available at https://lccn.loc.gov/2025016696
LC ebook record available at https://lccn.loc.gov/2025016697

ISBN 978-0-8091-5711-2 (paperback)
ISBN 978-0-8091-8866-6 (ebook)

Published by Paulist Press
997 Macarthur Boulevard
Mahwah, NJ 07430
www.paulistpress.com

Printed and bound in the
United States of America

Published in Canada by Novalis

Publishing Office   Head Office
1 Eglinton Avenue East, Suite 800   4475 Frontenac Street
Toronto, Ontario, Canada   Montréal, Québec, Canada
M4P 3A1   H2H 2S2
en.novalis.ca

Cataloguing in Publication is available from Library and Archives Canada.

ISBN: 978-2-89830-320-3

We acknowledge the support of the Government of Canada.

To Tom Penney:
colleague, intrepid pilgrim, ardent lover of all things Roman;
a joy to travel with; a specimen of synodality

What we really want is a total reorganization of society and the church.

James O'Gara, past editor of *Commonweal*, on the fiftieth anniversary of the Catholic magazine in 1973. Half a century later we may well be on the cusp of precisely such a radical undertaking, courtesy of Pope Francis and synodality.

CONTENTS

Acknowledgments ix

I. Prelude 1

II. The First Session: October 2023 37

III. The Interregnum 89

IV. The Second Session: October 2024 91

V. Epilogue 114

VI. Postlude: *Habemus Papam* 126

Notes 131

References 133

ACKNOWLEDGMENTS

N O WORK IS EVER the product of one person—it takes a company of folk to achieve the final outcome. It is the synodal way in action. Here follow some, but not all, of those folk for this book.

Donna Crilly and Bob Byrns are always there, at the beginning and at the end.

Paulist Press ensured that the credentials necessary from the Press Office of the Holy See were secured, enabling me to do my work on-site.

My daughter Sarah, a professional editor, assisted with the preparation of the text and my daughter Alexa, a professional researcher, facilitated the transcriptions.

Also deserving of great thanks: The support of the University of St. Michael's College, particularly that provided by its president, David Sylvester, has been invaluable and sustaining. The accommodations and lush generosity of the Generalate community of the Missionary Oblates of Mary Immaculate, in Rome, have few parallels. The work of Sacred Heart University (Fairfield, CT) in hosting immediate post-synodal forums for enlightened discussion was a major driver of lay involvement. Michelle Loris and Daniel Rober were critical in conceiving and executing these post-synodal virtual debates.

At the heart of this book is the act of listening and sharing. The many fecund conversations among such *illustrissimi* of Vatican journalists, scholars, commentators, reporters, and sage veterans as Colleen Dulle, Sebastien Gomes, Austen Ivereigh, Cathy Clifford, Elizabeth Davis, Natalie Becquart, Christopher Lamb, Christopher White, Mark O'Connor, and Tom Reese were and remain a highlight of the enterprise.

The guiding principle of the diary is to show the continuity between the Second Vatican Council and the papacy of Francis, and in so doing demonstrate the shared ecclesial vision of Roncalli and Bergoglio.

I have drawn on the research and writing of various of my previous columns and books, including those for *The Globe and Mail* (Toronto), *The Tablet* (London), and the *Synodal Times* (Dublin)—in addition to *The Church Needs the Laity: The Wisdom of John Henry Newman*, and chapter 8 of *The Jesuit Disruptor: A Personal Portrait of Pope Francis*, called "Ragging the Puck: Synodality Is the Apex."

The diary is an amuse-bouche and a prolegomenon. It is designed to introduce the reader to some of the players, themes, dramas, and conflicts that define the Synod on Synodality. More detailed, nuanced, and systematic studies by theologians and historians will appear in years to come, works delivered by accomplished experts in their respective fields.

In the meantime, the amuse-bouche.

I

PRELUDE

R OMAN EPISCOPAL SYNODS are rare phenomena in the history of the Roman Catholic Church. But not as rare as they once were. In fact, not that rare at all since 1969.

Drawn from the Greek word *synhodos*, which means "to walk or travel together," the structure of the synod has undergone significant changes over the centuries with many of those changes being of recent genesis.

My experience with synods has been restricted to the Roman episcopal synods held at the Vatican every few years. I was assigned the task of covering the now rightly celebrated Extraordinary Synod of 1985—the twentieth anniversary of the closing of the Second Vatican Council (SVC), a synod marked by surprising developments, decisions that would shape the Church for decades to come, internecine curial warfare, an international platform for emerging prelates of influence, and massive media coverage.

I was part of that coverage.

Assigned to report and analyze the public and private doings of the synod for *Grail: An Ecumenical Journal*, *Catholic New Times*, *The Toronto Star*, and the Canadian Broadcasting Corporation (CBC), I decided to do three things: publish the official texts, conduct interviews with as many players at the synod as would meet with me, and record my daily impression of the synod as it unfolded over the two weeks of its formal duration.

It is the diary format that is the heart of this book on the 2023–2024 Synod on Synodality. This is a sketchbook by a journalist and English literature professor, not a theologian's measured summary of the synodal proceedings. The latter is, of course, indispensable to a full appreciation of what unfolded at the synod—but it is not what I set out to do. I wanted to create a written gallimaufry: a potpourri of perceptions, characters, factions and tensions, intrigues and turmoils, epiphanies and graced moments of insight.

In short, in the words of the man who summoned the synod in the first place: a mess.

A diary is the most difficult to write, but the easiest to access for readers. I had very limited experience with keeping a diary or journal as a personal instrument of discovery and disclosure. I had considerable experience, however, studying diaries because of my doctoral work on the American monk-poet Thomas Merton, one of the giants of the genre of the last century. I knew as a scholar that diaries can be both exploratory and revelatory, both experimental and traditional, a record of the past—personal and experiential as well as detached and historical—and an instrument of prognostication.

The French Nobel Prize winner for literature, Annie Ernaux, collapses the difference between autobiography and fiction in her novels and writes compellingly that she "believe[s] that any experience, whatever its nature, has the inalienable right to be chronicled. There is no such thing as a lesser truth."[1]

Certainly, Merton subscribed to such a view. He wrote many diaries, meticulously chronicling his daily experiences and events as they happened. But they were also journals, seasoned and well-crafted personal observations that went beyond simply recording the impressions in their immediate context.

Another consummate diarist was the novelist Virginia Woolf, whose detailed and intimate diaries constitute a major portion of her impressive oeuvre as a writer. As Anne Chisholm—the editor of the letters of the decorative artist, painter, and the Bloomsbury Group contemporary of Woolf's, Dora Carrington—has observed of Woolf:

> For her, the diary was "practice....I do my scales." It was also where she could experiment, play with words and ideas and discharge uncomfortable emotions. As Adam Phillips [the British psychotherapist] puts it, she could "suspend her preoccupation with form...the anecdotal and sporadic and the impressionistic suited Woolf's sensibility." She could take risks, be "less tactful, less cautious, less continent."[2]

I certainly don't intend to limit myself to doing my scales—nor did I plan on being tactless, reckless, and incontinent as I crafted my diary. But I do hope some of these risky qualities seep through because a diary should be a textured undertaking, replete with probes, asides, subtexts, playful banter, and irreverent commentary: an honest intellectual portrait of a time, place, and event. Imperfect, of course, like its creator—but bold and theatrical in its way. After all, the dramatis personae of the synod are not colorless individuals, mere instruments of a process, silent witnesses to a momentous event. They are players.

Before I arrive, however, on the shores of the Tiber to engage in a mite of reportage regarding the Synod on Synodality, it would be helpful to give you some context. And in doing so, show how the synod once worked and how it now works, why the Francis Synod on Synodality is revolutionary as well as evolutionary, and

3

why the Extraordinary Synod of 1985 is pivotal to understanding why synods matter as ecclesiological events.

From November 24 to December 8, 1985, I attended the Extraordinary Synod of Catholic Bishops convened at the Vatican to "review" the twenty years that had elapsed since the conclusion of the momentous Second Vatican Council. It was strictly a bishops' event. Each national conference of bishops would send carefully chosen delegates who were empowered to deliver very short addresses, or interventions, in the synod hall on a postconciliar theme. After several days of these uninterrupted monologues—there was no engagement on the floor, no questions or sparks of conversation—they would then adjourn to their language-specific groups for *in camera* chats, reflections, and pious reminiscences. These small discussion assemblies, or *circuli minores*, held promise for some authentic dialogue, but whatever was said was confidential and the journalists were given scraps from the table, quickly composed summaries with no identifiers—and often no grammar—that only whetted the appetites of the scribblers. Very early on we were poised for battle: the struggle to wring the truth, any truth, from the participants, to get information that was more than tired ecclesiastical tropes, and to capture something of the fire of debate and personality that must surely have been surfacing somewhere.

I discovered that the alliterative lyricism of the Press Office of the Holy See—La Sala Stampa Della Santa Sede—belied the mundane chaos of its daily proceedings. The Press Office Bulletins were like runes that needed to be deciphered. When, for instance, the Sala Stampa issued a summary called the *relatio* of the report by the relator of the synod, the urbane and fluent cardinal archbishop of Malines-Brussels, Godfried Danneels, the official tasked with providing a summary of all the episcopal reports sent to Rome prior to the synod's convocation, the Press Bulletin managed to highlight the positive points the reports identified as

SVC achievements in such a way that was uniformly bland in the telling, when not crushingly self-evident.

The negative points were, by contrast, far less colorless, embroidered with passages of purple prose and redolent of an era of dramatic denunciations and anathemas: "horizontal reductionism," "moralizing cerebralism," "ethical subjectivism," a world of hoary ecclesiastical discourse.

At the first evening press briefing on the opening day of the synod, we were introduced to a convivial Dublin monsignor, Diarmuid Martin, who had a clear penchant for wordy summaries. It was clear that he liked his job never so more than when given a reprieve by a tired press corps from answering their importunate questions. He wanted us, implored us, to be satisfied with the bulletins at hand. He read the notes that he had taken of the eight-minute interventions delivered by the synod fathers that morning, a summarized recitation made necessary by the Vatican's reluctance to release the prepared texts. The Vatican felt that the general circulation of the interventions could compromise the speaker at home.

This practice, an easy invitation to scornful skepticism by those covering the synod for both the Catholic and secular media, made no sense. After all, if a bishop is fearful that what he says can place him in jeopardy (even though his intervention has already been through the clearinghouse of his own national episcopal conference), this is no remedy—there is no permanent guarantee of confidentiality anyway as the Sala Stampa will issue daily twenty-line summaries of the interventions, followed by Martin's own encapsulations at the nightly press briefings.

So why not make the texts available as they are, avoiding needless potential misrepresentations, all the while projecting an image of accountability? Little would have been lost, and much would have been gained. In fact, many of the interventions were made available beforehand by national episcopal conferences, although under embargo until delivered. But this was a practice characteristic of the English-speaking delegations and not universally adopted by other national bodies. And the official translation mechanisms were slow, labored, and often amateurish. Reporters and analysts had to rely on the tried-and-true SVC protocol of accessing pirated versions from bishops, accompanying *periti* (experts), and rogue Vatican communications officials.

I was learning fast. The Vatican's modus operandi for dealing with information was to restrict (not augment) access, controlling the content and the transmission of data with a master hand, invoking secrecy, and keeping at bay investigating and curious minds. The Vatican had yet to learn the wisdom of the towering Victorian Catholic historian Lord Acton, who opined that "everything secret degenerates, even the administration of justice; nothing is safe that does not show it can bear discussion and publicity."

Given the synod's method of proceeding, there was a delicious irony in the press bulletin of November 26, 1985, quoting Archbishop John Foley's intervention wherein he said, "Some Catholic publications feature dissent more than dogma, while some Church spokespersons show unnecessary secrecy, defensiveness and fear of the truth." A former editor of a Philadelphia archdiocesan newspaper, inveterate opera lover, the face of the Vatican's outreach to film companies and documentarians—as I discovered when working on a series on the Vatican—and the then-president of the Pontifical Commission for Social Communications, Foley's misinterpretation of what a Catholic publication should be and his tepid reprimand of closeted Vatican communications policy highlight the contradictions that beset the institution when its approach to releasing substantive materials is informed by fear and constraint with only a patina of openness.

As the synod proceeded into the second week with the delegates arranged in their language-designated discussion groups, or *circuli minores*, the press briefings promised to offer more by way of information. But it was not to be.

Prelude

The press briefings consisted largely of cursory outlines—not substantive content—of the *circuli minores*. The daily bulletins summarizing the discussions were produced with an unfathomable speed and indicated the difficulties that came from having to condense and synthesize the wealth of material and comment generated. The language and format were reminiscent of the minutes one would take of a meeting: noncontroversial, studied neutrality, tiresome recapitulation.

Both the discussions, as recorded in the published summaries, and Martin's briefings echoed the early interventions of the bishops. The summaries become devoid of the potential electricity of conflict, allowing no disagreement to surface. All is perfect unity to those outside the enclave of bishops. That is the impression the Sala Stampa is determined to ensure is the public face of the synod.

As a consequence, the press, ever alert to the slightest quiver of controversy, alights on any issue that may vibrate with the prospect of fire, any fire, no matter how meagre or fantastical. The results of this kind of media desperation are easily seen: issues and ideas suffer from a proper lack of focus and proportionality.

A perfect example of the farcical search for facticity at this 1985 synod, with its entrenched culture of controlled releases, muffled voices, and oppressive secrecy, occurred in the second week when it was rumored that a letter from an unspecified number of Latin American cardinals professing both their loyalty to the pope and their unhesitating repudiation of the theology of liberation had surfaced in the Spanish edition of the Vatican official newspaper, *L'Osservatore Romano*. The formidable director of Sala Stampa, the Opus Dei physician, surgeon, journalist, and social communications expert Dr. Joaquín Navarro-Valls, denied that there ever was such a letter, noting only that a Mexican cardinal in his intervention spoke of those matters to be found in the elusive non-letter. At lunch with the eminent journalist and papal biographer Peter Hebblethwaite, the Australian Vaticanista Desmond O'Grady, and John Wilkins, editor of *The Tablet* (London),

I discovered that the copy O'Grady had of the now much-coveted Spanish edition quoting the letter was missing something: The "non-letter" on page eight of *L'Osservatore Romano* had been mysteriously snipped. And not by O'Grady's hand.

A ruse, a plot, a frantic bit of wild news-making?

Moving inexorably toward the crafting of a pastoral synod message that they had agreed to make—this is separate from John Paul II's own meditation on the fruits of the synod proceedings, which were published after all was consummated—Martin had to preside over an uncharacteristically tumultuous gathering.

Chaos, pettiness, rude cajoling, loud jeering ensued—a mad cacophony of sounds and gestures that I hadn't experienced yet in the Stampa's briefing room. It was rather exciting to see such high feelings after nearly two weeks of controlled agenda, expert evasional tactics, and opacity around the pro and contra forces at work in a synod called to review the state of the Church two decades after the end of an ecumenical council.

Martin was incapable of restoring a measure of order, and his press briefing deteriorated rapidly. This was the cost of a fortnight of simmering frustration. He had no news of substance to offer and feelings ran high. After all, the world's media was on-site. The number of print and broadcast journalists assigned by both secular and religious media to cover the synod actually exceeded those present at all four sessions of the SVC. No subsequent synod during the papacies of John Paul II and Benedict XVI would command more than a small fraction of the media attention accorded the Extraordinary Synod of 1985.

This was the synod to cover. It was my debut as an amateur Vaticanista, and it was the ideal portal through which to pass to get a close familiarity with the way things are done and to taste firsthand the utter inadequacies of the Vatican communications machinery in dealing with democratic notions of media freedom, transparency, accountability, and the values of investigative rigor.

The synod exploded on the theological scene in some key

defining ways, but it also exploded on the media scene in ways that would shape a generation of coverage.

But prelates and journalists can change, as I discovered with Martin. The once-effervescent evader in time became a staunch advocate of transparency and full communication.

Dublin changed him.

Attached to various bodies in Geneva and elsewhere on human rights issues, Martin was eventually appointed archbishop of Dublin at a particularly gruesome time for the Irish Church. Desmond Connell, a previous cardinal-archbishop and Maynooth metaphysician, was media-hostile, or at least uncomprehending of its mission. Calls for the release of files on clerical sex abuse—past and present—during his administration mounted relentlessly. He was overwhelmed by the range and unprecedented nature of the clerical sex abuse crisis and became obsessively protective of what he considered confidential personnel files. He failed to grasp the magnitude of the issue for the Irish Church.

Martin's response was very different from all his living predecessors. He opened the files of retired auxiliary bishops who had either been tainted by scandal or who were inept, or disciplined priests who were legitimately accused, and acted with such speed and impartiality that many came to see him as a ruthless scourge who had little time for sensitive pastoral attention.

While I was the president of St. Thomas University in Fredericton, New Brunswick, I had invited Martin to receive an honorary doctorate with Nobel Peace Prize winner and Northern Ireland politician John Hume. We visited Saint John, New Brunswick's provincial capital, so that the archbishop could address the Irish community of the province, and I listened as he firmly insisted that his communications officer back in Dublin persist with Martin's increasingly firm entreaties that Connell comply with the law and release the personnel files. No bargains, no exceptions, no deference.

Full transparency. No longer a Vatican media apparatchik but a shepherd struggling to restore a modicum of credible authority to the bedraggled, and sometimes disgraced, Irish hierarchy, Martin came to prize what he had earlier feared: candor and openness.

Although candor and openness were not synodal qualities in 1985 for the bishop-delegates as well as the Vatican press mandarins, what was in clear evidence were conflicting ecclesiologies reluctant to surface in the presence of a pontiff with a reputation for playing a strong hand.

On the surface, as John Paul II said in his allocution at the synod's conclusion, there were three particular themes or concerns running through the two-week synod: the universal need for a compendium of Church teachings (in other words, a catechism), a study of the true nature of episcopal conferences, and the rapid conclusion of the Code of Canon Law for the Eastern Churches. There were other themes, and there was a lot of drama afoot—if veiled from the scrutinizing eyes of the media—that belied the pontiff's assertion that the synod reflected *complete unanimity* to the world.

If only.

The almost compulsive need to show the world a unified face meant that the synod massaged the message, deflected any attention from possible or real areas of collision of view and personality, and in the process perverted the true nature of ecclesial unity. This was perhaps best illustrated by the high level of defensiveness around the role of John Paul II during the synod: his motivation for calling the synod in the first place, his strategy of restoration reclaiming the *ancien régime* from the postconciliar distorters, his reassertion of papal power through a highly centralized governance oversight, his deep suspicion of reformers and dissidents, and more. In great part this portrait of Karol Wojtyla is a caricature; his intention in summoning the synod was to celebrate, examine, promote, and assess the rich insights and values of the Second Vatican Council. It was not to undermine its credibility and validity—no pope, no matter how obscurantist, can do that—and it was not conceived of as a Metternich-like recovery of the old order.

Still, the synod did manage to create deep suspicions around John Paul II's purpose behind calling it in the first place. In doing so it underscored the problems inherent in a church structure that feared open dialogue, obsessed about clerical control, mismanaged communication with the media, encouraged a climate of hypercaution among attending prelates, and, when dealing with those outside the synod, exercised a heightened reserve.

Those suspicious critics of John Paul's plan for the synod were harboring dangerous thoughts delighted in listening to the words of the cardinal archbishop of Dakar, Hyacinthe Thiandoum, who thundered (in content darkly if not in delivery loudly), "Is it not more surprising, I must say almost scandalous, that an agitation, without any basis, determined, in spite of objectives so clearly defined by one whose fidelity to Vatican II is known to everyone, to place this Synod and its promoter in opposition to the Second Vatican Council itself?"

The cardinal's deploring of the "agitation" was misdirected. The failure to publicly recognize the existence of different points of view loyally expressed, thereby reducing all criticism to maligned assaults on the pontiff, resulted in a misreading of the synod fathers, whose already muted critiques were honest expressions of opinion.

It took Bishop Georges Singha of the Congo to remind the delegates, in his intervention, of one of the salient truths of the council, that "unity is not a synonym for uniformity, nor standardization, nor levelling, but must go hand-in-hand with diversity, differences, variety and perhaps multiplicity."

Although the design of the synod from the outset was to constitute an ongoing diagnosis of the SVC's impact on current Church life and to do so in a way that did not repudiate the council and its teachings, it should not have come as a surprise to anyone that diverse perspectives would, and *should*, surface.

Debates over the liberation theology movement that originated in Latin America with its various academic and political-ecclesiastical personalities—Gustavo Gutiérrez, Ernesto Cardenal, Clodovis Boff, Jon Sobrino, Juan-Luis Segundo, Pedro Casaldáliga, Hélder Câmara—loomed large at the synod, though it was not officially an item on the synodal agenda.

But the personality that loomed larger than any was the prefect of the Congregation for the Doctrine of the Faith, Cardinal Joseph Ratzinger. He was the presiding eminence of the proceedings, the Vatican's own attack dog.

Just prior to the synod, the *Rapporto sulla Fede—The Ratzinger Report*—was published in English, and it created a windstorm of controversy. A series of interviews conducted with Italian journalist Vittorio Messori, *The Ratzinger Report* does not pull its punches. The cardinal laments what he calls "the hermeneutic of rupture," the corrosive impact on the life of the Church by what is often dubbed the "spirit of Vatican II," and the general decline of reverence for, if not belief in, the central doctrines of the Church and its devotional life.

The book was a blistering attack—one wag likened it to a turbocharged cleansing of the sinuses—as the synod delegates would have been only too aware of the book's impact, its forthright content, and the abiding presence of its author during their extraordinary episcopal assembly.

The key item in *The Ratzinger Report* that surfaced on the synod floor was the status, canonical and theological, of episcopal conferences. Ratzinger feared the political dynamics of such a body: the undermining of the individual responsibility of the local bishop, or Ordinary; the prevalence of groupthink; the fallacious assumption that such an organization could "vote on truth" as if it were a parliamentary structure.

The American bishop James Malone, the then-president of the United States Conference of Catholic Bishops, defended the conference as an "expression of collegiality"—collegiality being the principle that affirms the collaboration and co-responsibility of the college of bishops with its head Peter as "the first among equals" or *primus inter pares.*

The Jesuit Church historian John O'Malley situates episcopal collegiality within the context of the Dogmatic Constitution of the Church, *Lumen Gentium*, the foundational document of the Second Vatican Council itself, and in so doing highlights its continuing importance:

> The lightning-rod issue at the council was episcopal collegiality. No other section of any other [council] document was more contested or received more minute scrutiny than chapter 3 ["The Hierarchical Structure of the Church and in Particular on the Episcopate"] of *Lumen Gentium.* Even after the council overwhelmingly approved that chapter, the issue did not die but returned at the last moment in the famous *Nota praevia* attached to the decree by "a higher authority." The fierce and unrelenting opposition to collegiality from a small but powerful minority at the council...indicates that something important was at stake, something more than an updating or a development.[3]

The controversy around collegiality did not abate; it continued underground in most cases until it reappeared at the '85 Synod in full view. Malone had support from several bishops, most notably from John Gran, bishop emeritus of Oslo and president of the Nordic Bishops' Conference, who spiritedly reminded the synod that the doctrine of collegiality failed to fructify according to expectations. But there were many who stood against Malone's position that episcopal conferences can be a means of collegiality. He remained committed, however, bolstering his argument by noting in his intervention that democracy, the hydra feared by many of the curialists and *Ratzinger Report* aficionados, is one of the "wholesome values and procedures from our culture [that can] serve ecclesial communion and the proclamation of the gospel of Jesus Christ, just as well as the wholesome values and procedures of any other people and culture."

In this he was foreshadowed by the Canadian bishops' response to the questionnaire sent out prior to the synod by the General Secretariat of the Synod, the body responsible for orchestrating the management, preparation, and running of the synod—a response that was clandestinely delivered to the editors of Montreal's *Le Devoir*: "It seems too easy to completely oppose collegiality or democratic tendencies in all forms on the basis that the church is a divine institution. The Synod should clearly reaffirm its support of collegiality and own the consequences of collegiality in the life of the church."

Easier said than done.

Malone had opposition from Ratzinger's friend, the conservative cardinal archbishop of Philadelphia, John Krol, who at a press conference acknowledged that national episcopal conferences could be a "useful and necessary collaborative pastoral initiative," but they are not "an instrument of collegiality."

There were many debates—sometimes aggravatingly oblique and offstage—that erupted throughout the '85 Synod and are only now being fully enjoined by the 2023–2024 Synod on Synodality. Because now we have Francis with his love of *parrhesia* (free speaking in the Spirit) guaranteeing a different experience of synod. I have not had the opportunity yet to attend a Bergoglio-inspired synod, although I have followed the synodal process and documents they produced in the previous synods he summoned.

The seeds were planted in 1985 and the full flowering is now in 2023.

But the Extraordinary Synod of 1985 was not the first synod of the Catholic Church. In fact, synods—gatherings of bishops—had been convoked many times over the centuries to deal with issues of doctrine, ecclesial order, as well as matters of discipline.

Some four hundred synods of various hues and colors were held between the middle of the second century CE up to the pontificate of Gregory I (590–604). As Jesuit theologian T. Howland Sanks notes:

> This conciliar or synodal tradition did not cease with the early church but continued as the main form of decision-making. It was also the expression of unity of the various local churches who understood themselves as a *communio communiorum*, a communion of communions.[4]

Although there would be various debates and movements throughout the later Middle Ages up to the nineteenth century about the nature of episcopal collegiality, papal primacy, Roman universal jurisdiction, and "conciliarism"—a notion that, among other things, insisted on a universal Church council as superior in authority over the Bishop of Rome—by the time of the First Vatican Council in 1869–1870 under the reactionary Pio Nono or Pius IX the matter appeared settled in favor of an infallible pontiff, even if that infallibility was rarely exercised and even then under tight restrictions. The synodal path was not on the books.

When it returned in the Second Vatican Council it was still a highly delicate, if not tetchy, issue. The Council fathers made it clear that they wanted to enhance the relationship they had with the Bishop of Rome, undoubtedly as a consequence of the liberating experience they had of collegiality at the council. Why not continue this into the future, they reasoned.

And so, while working on the document on the bishops' pastoral office in the Church (*Christus Dominus*), they made the case that the Church should make the provision for an ongoing gathering of the universal College of Bishops with delegates representing the global hierarchy. However, before their suggestion could be acted on, Paul VI issued the *motu proprio* (*Apostolica*

Sollicitudo) whereby he established the Synod of Bishops, took pains to define its nature, scope, and authority, and essentially took the discussion out of the council *aula* to make the synod a creation of papal *fiat*. This is not the only occasion when Pope Paul made the decision to take controverted matters off the council agenda, thereby reserving for himself as successor of Peter the resolution he sought. It should be said that he did these things not because he was controlling and manipulative but because he feared division and was by nature inclined to *Hamletismo*, or exaggerated introspection.

Regardless, the Church now had a new central ecclesiastical institute, although debates raged—in a subterranean way— around whether the synod was an extension of the Roman curia, in which collegiality is defined simply in terms of an advisory role and not as a collegial act of the College of Bishops itself. As a consequence of these debates, the College's decision-making and influence were limited.

Canon lawyer and bishop emeritus Anthony Tonnos sees the synod created by Paul VI as a true exercise of the College of Bishops, "either in a wide sense—those participating do so by virtue of their membership in the episcopal college and not as delegates of the pope—or, even in the strict sense of genuinely collegial action, since there is nothing to preclude a strictly collegial act from being conducted in a representative manner. *Christus Dominus*...signifies that all the bishops in hierarchical communion participate in solicitude for the universal Church."[5]

The reintroduction or reinstitution of the synod as a means of governance, however circumscribed and although hailed as a good thing, was never going to be an entirely satisfactory recovery. It needed fixing from the outset. Although the synod is seen as a collaborative exercise between the universal episcopate and the Bishop of Rome, the terms of actual operation, the agenda or theme, and the senior oversight appointments—president-delegates and the key figures in the Secretariat of the Synod—are exclusively papal appointments. Dominique Le Tourneau breaks it down:

> The Roman pontiff convenes the synod whenever it seems to him to be opportune. He decides on the questions to be dealt with as well as the order of the day, ratifies the choice of members to be elected and the regulation of the synod, and at times presides in person over the sessions.[6]

In short, the pope has a disproportionate role in the proceedings of the synod up to and including the summary and final report. Although it is true that the synodal fathers have a clear say in many of the appointments and are not a negligible factor when it comes to the formulation of the documents that appear at the end of the synod itself, the key driver remains the Supreme Pontiff.

In the beginning, this sort of arrangement made sense. But as time unfolded and the practice on the ground of many of the synods, both Ordinary and Extraordinary, indicated the flaws in the process—despite the tinkering Benedict XVI deployed in trying to make the synod a smoother and more collegial exercise—it was Francis who actually began the synodal reform necessary to make it a vital and credible instrument of governance and universal reflection.

And he did this in great part by insisting on *parrhesia*, or freely speaking in the Spirit without intimidation by authority, thereby ensuring that candid discussion was the order of the day. This was emphatically not the normal practice at the synods that preceded Francis's pontificate. Many bishop-delegates spoke off the record about the constraints they experienced at the synods, the heavy redaction of their discussions in the *circuli minores*, the artificial collegiality experienced in the synod hall when they gave their interventions, and the straitjacketing of their views in the final propositions.

Of course, much of this behavior is easily attributable to any governance structure—think of the overt as well as subtle politicking behind the scenes of parliaments, senates, and congresses around the world when it comes to controlling the directions of both consultative and deliberative committees or bodies—but a Church assembly, a synod of bishops, is not primarily a political body. It is a gathering engaged in prayerfully and honestly discerning, in light of the synodal topic and employing the best of the Church's thinking and pastoral instincts, the best responses of the universal Church to the challenges of the day.

Pope Francis encountered a wall of timidity rather than a wave of temerity when he convoked his own synods. But he was resolute. In fact, as Francis's biographer Paul Vallely writes:

> Pope Francis has said he plans to make changes to the international Synod of Bishops to make it more collegial, as Vatican II intended. That intention had been undermined by the insistence of Benedict XVI, when he was head of the Congregation for the Doctrine of the Faith, that episcopal conferences "had no theological significance," being mere collections of bishops whose collective weight was theologically no more than the sum of their parts. By contrast Francis told the fifteen-member coordinating council of the synod in June 2013: "We trust that the Synod of Bishops will be further developed to better facilitate dialogue and collaboration of the bishops among themselves and with the Bishop of Rome."[7]

This was more than papal boilerplate. He cast down the gauntlet. He was serious about collegiality, he was serious about synodality, and he was serious about implementing these principles in the life of the Church in meaningful rather than symbolic ways.

Prelude

The synod structure that Francis inherited—though permanent—was not in its particulars and process inured to change. Francis was convinced that it needed jets of oxygen, that it was often an intellectually airless chamber, its participants engaged more in rote and cautious vocabulary than in bold and dynamic interchanges both among themselves and with the pope. It was a propitious time for change.

Prior to Francis's election in 2013, following the startling and unpredictable resignation of Benedict XVI, the Church had hosted sixteen Ordinary Synods, two Extraordinary Synods, and ten Special Synods. The Ordinary Synods are scheduled to be held at specifically determined intervals, are universal rather than regional in their focus, are primarily pastoral in emphasis, and are distinctly contemporary rather than historical in their hermeneutical lens. Extraordinary Synods have greater urgency driving them and, though highly limited in their number and constitution by comparison with the Ordinary Synods, are more explicitly theological and ecclesiological in their nature. Special Synods are geographically limited and specific to a Church in a particular region: Africa, America, Asia, Europe, Oceania, the Netherlands, Lebanon, and Amazonia.

Francis's synodal record includes two Ordinary Synods to date: the 2015 "The Vocation and Mission of the Family in the Church and in the Contemporary World," with the resulting Apostolic Exhortation *Amoris Laetitia* (The Joy of Love), and the 2018 "Young People, Faith and Vocational Discernment," with the resulting apostolic exhortation *Christus Vivit* (Christ Lives). He also convoked one Extraordinary Synod, the 2014 "Pastoral Challenges of the Family in the Context of Evangelization," and one Special Synod on the Pan-Amazon Region in 2019 with the Apostolic Exhortation *Querida Amazonia* (Beloved Amazon Region).

Both these synods raised issues of great import for the Church and generated controversy both within synod halls and in the Church at large. Chancery personnel were ruffled, canon lawyers vexed, theological purists upstaged, and a level and volume of excitement created that no previous synod had ever managed, or even wished, to create.

New pope, new synods.

To make sure that future synods conformed to a different model—not radically different, but different and enhanced—and to set in place a template that publicly guaranteed a synod grounded in a truly conciliar perspective, Francis issued in 2018 an apostolic exhortation on the Synod of Bishops, *Episcopalis Communio* (Episcopal Communion).

The document was the result of incorporating the reflections and analyses by theologians on the topic of "synodality in the life of the church" and became the foundation stone on which would be built a "constitutively synodal church." Although the bishop-delegates would in no way be supplanted, they would be complemented, as consultations with the faithful and indeed participation by the laity would become the new normal in a declericalized Church. Francis emphasized that the bishops, including specifically the Bishop of Rome, were disciples called to listen "to the voice of Christ speaking through the entire people of God."

And *listening* is the operative word. Cardinal Michael Czerny, SJ, agrees:

> The keystone is listening: every synodal praxis "begins by listening to the people of God," "continues by listening to the pastors" and culminates in listening to the Bishop of Rome, called to declare himself "Pastor and Doctor of all Christians."...*Episcopalis Communio* divided synodal praxis into three phases: preparation, discussion and implementation, and each Synod celebrated during the current pontificate—on the family (2014, 2015), on young people (2018), on the Amazon (2019)—has sought to implement these phases to an

increasing extent. As the Holy Father has observed, "the changes introduced so far go in the direction of making the Synods held every two or three years in Rome freer and more dynamic, giving more time for sincere discussion and listening."[8]

There is no doubt—considering the Francis synods to date—that he has succeeded in making these gatherings "freer and more dynamic." Respectfully, the previous synods, in my experience, were neither free nor dynamic and their impact on the life of the Church accordingly reduced to general irrelevance. The bishops had their own legitimate, if constrained, experience of collegiality under tight Roman supervision, but the larger communion of Catholics had no taste of the experience, save that mediated by their bishops following their return from the synod. And that mediation varied massively depending on the local bishop's buy-in, the commitment to translating and transmitting the synod proceedings through the agencies of the national episcopal conferences or by means of the bishop-delegates themselves through their own outreach.

Not a satisfactory method of operating.

Francis's way of "synodizing" is essentially an overturning of the previous way of operating. Biographer and Bergoglio scholar Austen Ivereigh captures the radicality of it all when he says,

Not only was the synod now a permanent central body, separated from the Roman Curia and subject directly to the bishops and the pope, but it was recognized as having the authority to teach and steer the universal Church under the guidance of the Holy Spirit. For anyone who is familiar with the modern Church, this was an astonishing development. Rather than waiting for a Roman dicastery to close off discussion, the synod in

Rome was a means of opening it....That made it powerful, because "power is something that is shared,"
he told *El País*, adding: "Power exists when we make
decisions that have been mediated, talked about, and
prayed over."[9]

This is utterly consonant with the thinking of John Henry
Newman, the English cardinal and thinker whom Francis canon-
ized early in his pontificate. Newman had said in his seminal *On
Consulting the Faithful in Matters of Doctrine* (1859), concerning
the role of the laity, that

> I think certainly that the *Ecclesia docens* [the Church as
> teacher or Magisterium] is more happy when she has
> such enthusiastic partisans about her...than when she
> cuts off the faithful from the study of her divine doc-
> trines and the sympathy of her divine contemplations,
> and requires from them a *fides implicita* in her word,
> which in the educated classes will terminate in indif-
> ference, and in the poorer in superstition.[10]

Francis would have no difficulty agreeing with Newman's
argument that "truth is wrought out by many minds, working
together freely." Newman believed in the vital and free interplay
of intellect and authority, of freedom and discipline in a way that
assured the necessity of both—ever poised in tension, but ever-
struggling to apprehend the deepest truth. Newman, in his autobiography *Apologia pro Vita Sua*, provides the Roman Catholic
postconciliar Church with a model of such exquisite balance and
utter reasonableness that one cannot but be pained by our contemporary atmosphere of toxic mistrust, visceral broadsides
against the pontiff, and *argumentum ad hominem* polemics with
little regard for facts and tolerance, all opening ever-deeper fis-

sures in the communion of Christ. Here is what Newman says of the Church:

> It is a vast assemblage of human beings with willful intellects and wild passions, brought together into one by the beauty and the Majesty of a Superhuman Power, into what may be called a large reformatory or training-school, not as if into a hospital or prison, not in order be sent to bed, not to be buried alive, but (if I may change metaphor) brought together as if into some moral factory, for the melting, refining, and molding, by an incessant noisy process, of the raw material, so excellent, so dangerous, so capable of divine purposes.[11]

Admittedly, it is a relief to see Newman switch his metaphor and concentrate on the "melting, refining, and molding by an incessant noisy process," because that is precisely what acting synodally means. It is loud, cacophonous sometimes, spirited, a mess—all that human engagement with different cultural backgrounds, histories, hopes, and resistances cannot but be part din, part Babel, but also "a vast assemblage of human beings" struggling together to discern the truth, debating with conviction, discerning in the Spirit, and listening, listening.

The listening is the prelude to conversion—individual and ecclesial. As the cardinal archbishop of Newark, New Jersey, Joseph Tobin, rightly identifies, the larger context in which synodality is rendered concrete in the lives of Catholics and in the renewal or revitalizing of the Church's structures of mediation depends on an experience of conversion:

> We cannot deny that for centuries the Church has used synodality [however historically defined] as a way to kick people out. With every early ecumenical council, we would come together to repudiate this heresy or to

define that dogma, and the Body of Christ would lumber on. But I submit we have entered a new stage of the journey. Acts of synodality no longer function as sweeping dogmatic declarations, but rather are used to fine-tune how the Gospel is applied to the signs of the times. And with that comes the next important point of Francis's long game [following on synodality *as* journey]: conversion. When I say "conversion," I'm talking about the Church's own conversion, a new way in understanding and approaching how we carry out our mission. Francis has rightly decried the mindset of "But we've always done it this way." John XXIII famously said that we in the Church are not called to guard a museum but to tend to a flourishing garden of life. The same goes for a synodal Church. You can't show up with an imperious attitude, as if you have all the answers. Indeed, John XXIII read the signs of turmoil and destruction of the first half of the twentieth century and saw that the Church had to be as intentional and missionary as it possibly could with its witness—and that the way to achieve this was through a council.[12]

From the outset, Francis was determined to do something with the synod structure he inherited. Abolishing it was not in the cards, but strengthening it was. And to strengthen means for Francis finding a way of making it—the process of acting synodally—a more inclusive, free, and dialogue-friendly gathering wherein delegates speak their minds, without fear of a punitive response from the senior authorities when they go off script. After all, the scrum-loving Francis has set a model for candid and no-holds-barred speaking with his airplane press Q&A, and his easy departure from his prepared speeches giving ample room to spontaneity and inspiration—and generating ample nervousness among his script-adhering aides.

And so it is that with the Synod on Synodality, which after all is the subject of this book, the full universal implications of being a synodal Church are to be fathomed with a new freedom. All the previous Francis synods were not simply preparatory, as they had specific, pastoral as well as practical goals. And in this way they lay the groundwork for the Synod on Synodality with its theme of *Communion, Participation, and Mission.*

The three-year synodal process involves three phases: diocesan, continental, and universal. And it is the universal that is this diary's focus. Cardinal Archbishop of Vienna Christoph Schönborn, a member of the Council for the Synod of Bishops and a key player at the 1985 Extraordinary Synod, neatly summarizes the synodal process and its theological, catechetical, and pedagogical underpinnings in an interview with François Vayne for *Jerusalem Cross*:

> The Pope tells us that the Synod is not simply a procedure, a strategy towards a common goal. Synodality is more than that; its purpose is not about pastoral administration or social commitment. What we are being offered is, above all, the experience of the Holy Spirit, as in the New Testament, especially the Acts of the Apostles. During this great ecclesial time, we are all invited to experience reciprocal listening and encounter in the breath of the Holy Spirit, to better discern what God is asking of us today...it is a historical phase as important for the Church as that of the Second Vatican Council, but with a communal and universal dimension, a form of global Gospel School open to all.[13]

Schönborn's identification of the synod as a gospel school is a reminder that the synodal process is not something alien to the Catholic tradition, the reckless insertion into ecclesial affairs of a way of being better suited to a parliamentary democracy, but a school in which, through "reciprocal learning," the entire Church body comes together irrespective of office or rank to discern the will of the Holy Spirit for our time. Schools are ideally places of joy and playfulness, places of free time for the disinterested pursuit of the deeper mysteries of our existence. The Church as school is a place of ambient tenderness, a caring sanctuary where the person is treasured as a person and the little things that define our humanity are celebrated: being solicitous of someone having a bad day, holding the door for a stranger, smiling when encountering the downcast, paying attention to others by shattering our self-insulating bubble. It is also a place where a gentle and not pugilistic openness to dialogue can flourish, where a healthy engagement with the ideas of another is not license to excoriate. The Church as school is a place, a social gathering where polarizing rhetoric is not the norm and where scoring nasty and brutalizing points on your dialogue partner is discouraged. And the Church as school is a humanizing reality—not a factory, corporation, or ideological structure keen on monitoring conformity.

Although the selling job on why we need a synodal Church is still very much in its infancy—overcoming the comfortable status quo with its perks and settled certainties is never an easy task—Francis is moving forward confident that it is the Spirit that summons, that Catholics are yearning for a Church alive to human need and accompaniment, and that modelling via experience will be more successful than a cohort of academic symposia and a cascade of curial decrees.

The bishop of Brownsville, Texas, Daniel E. Flores, understands the synod as

> an enactment that accomplishes great good just in the act of gathering and listening, something simple, something eminently responsive to the love we have received in Christ. Building up our communion is not separate from engaging the mission to the nations,

because the witness of this love is essentially what our woundedness seems to need most.[14]

The notion of this kind of synod—a Francis synod—did not originate in the Bergoglio noggin *in vacuo*, synod delegate and theologian Catherine E. Clifford argues in "The Remedy of Synodality":

> The most radical of the remedies that Francis proposes for the renewal of the church and its mission is in his invitation to rediscover how to live as a more synodal church...the desire for a new culture of synodality is not just a personal wish, but by leading the church in this direction, he is carrying forward a mandate entrusted to him by his brother bishops, one forged in the sometimes-raucous exchanges among the members of the College of Cardinals preceding the conclave of election in the spring of 2013.[15]

If the synod that Francis is promoting is the result of his attentive listening to his brother bishops, it is a testament to his even deeper listening to the Church at large. And that is why he went further than the previous practice of simply inviting lay guests as auditors; he instituted further changes in the synod's composition by allowing for the participation of seventy non-bishop members—ten from each of the seven global conferences—mandating that young people be included and that a clear percentage of those named be women.

And he went further still: he granted the right to vote to all the delegates of the synod—lay and clerical, men and women, old and young. A global synod will have the face of the globe about it—anguished, yearning, troubled, and prayerful: the modern face of humanity in the concrete, not cast in abstraction and ideology.

During the "diocesan phase," much depended on the local ecclesiastical jurisdiction, the willingness of the Ordinary to invest time, personnel, money, and personal interest in gathering consultants, conducting questionnaires, holding parish sessions as well as diocesan sessions, and preparing thoughtful summaries for submission to the national bodies and Rome.

Some bishops took the call seriously and engaged passionately in an effort to make this Francis project work. A few complied with the General Secretariat for the synod's requests with the barest minimum investment and, arguably, the majority did more but with little in the way of energy, never entirely persuaded of the synod's potential efficacy and relevance. The majority remain the quiet doubters, but they can be brought onside once the synodal dynamic unfolds. Once they are persuaded that the synod is not a radical remaking of the Church that they know and that their leadership credibility is not on the line, and once they can see that the summons to gather is designed to provide a lived experience of a genuinely listening Church and is not in the end a structural threat but the revivification of the Second Vatican Council's multiple pastoral and theological insights, then they can see the challenges ahead and not be daunted or reduced to cynicism.

Added to the official diocesan responses—and in many ways more potent and creative in their conception and delivery—is the work of numerous bodies of independent and committed Catholics working with their diverse networks that are cross-diocesan in their reach. Going beyond the limited horizon of the questionnaires, choosing intentionally to go deeper into the causes behind those forces and attitudes that work against rather than for the Church of Jesus Christ, many of these unofficial groupings that pepper the body ecclesiastical issued their own reports, whether as addenda to formal diocesan responses to Rome or as discrete submissions.

The *Summary Report of the Catholic Network for Women's*

Equality—Embodying a Listening, Inclusive, Synodal Church—is a model example of the genre. In a section titled "A Synodal Church Recognizes the Inherent Dignity and Equality of Women as Equal Disciples in Ministry and Leadership," the document's authors write:

> With gratitude for the work of feminist biblical scholars and archaeologists, we have learned that co-responsibility is not a new idea. Jesus had women disciples and there also were prominent women in ministry and leadership in the early Church....We look forward to the day when women and men, according to their gifts, will collaborate in preaching, presiding, and administering sacraments in parishes, when Catholic women and men will work cooperatively in leadership roles at diocesan, national and international levels, and when women and men together will shape Catholic teaching and structures of governance in a synodal Church.

There were many organizations running a parallel, although not counter, synod—exploring with a freedom devoid of clerical constraint, institutional limitations, and established protocols the issues of compelling concern for them as women in the Church.

Although this all may have a ring of the liberal boilerplate about it, Catholic lay groups deeply unhappy with their Church leadership over numerous issues—rarely doctrinal, mostly disciplinary, and often related to clerical sex scandals—have been a feature of Catholic life since at least the Cardinal Hans Hermann Groër affair of 1990s Austria. Out of crisis is born new visioning or desperate retreat; the former revivifies and the latter entombs.

The issues raised by the various Catholic lay groups advocating for change and reform surfaced not only at the diocesan phase but at the continental as well. The work of the North American Working Group is especially noteworthy. Consisting of nine experts drawn from across the United States and Canada, it conducted detailed interviews covering every conceivable issue on the social justice and ecclesial terrain: Hispanic marginalization, drug addiction, homelessness, Christians in the public square, Indigenous isolation, structural obstacles to the full emancipation of women's gifts in society and in the Church, and many more besides. Their final report, *Doing Theology from the Existential Peripheries*, underscores through its extensive interviews, sociological data sifted through a theological prism, and on-the-ground experience admixed with refined theological analysis, the clear perspective of the pope:

> As Pope Francis teaches in *Veritatis Gaudium* (The Joy of Truth) theology should not provide pre-packaged answers and ready-made solutions, rather theologians should go to unfamiliar sites with risks and fidelity to the borderline. Theologians, Pope Francis observes, by going out to the peripheries are like "spiritual ethnographers" with the smell of the sheep, whose encounter with people in their cultures, histories, and sites of pain and hope will bring about an inward transformation as they seek for a "hermeneutic of integration" in accounting for the logic of grace and of the signs of God's reign from these sites.[16]

Building on such reports as the above with their impressive interview density, as well as reports that scan the entire globe and were received by the General Secretariat of the Synod, a working document for the Continental Stage was produced with the deliciously biblical title of *Enlarge the Space of Your Tent*. As it states,

> Globally, participation exceeded all expectations. In all, the Synod Secretariat received contributions from

112 out of 114 Episcopal Conferences and from all the
15 Oriental Catholic churches, plus reflections from
17 out of 23 dicasteries of the Roman Curia besides
those from religious superiors, from institutes of consecrated life and societies of apostolic life, and from
association and lay movements of the faithful. In
addition, over a thousand contributions arrived from
individuals and groups as well as insights gathered
through social media thanks to the initiative of the
Digital Synod.

The report includes content that can be turgid and yet also
arrestingly direct and personal. For instance, quoting a submission from Argentina, the pope's home country, the report bluntly
calls for a remodeling of ecclesial governance in keeping with the
Argentine pontiff's fondness for the inverted pyramid:

It is important to build a synodal institutional model
as an ecclesial paradigm of deconstructing pyramidal
power that privileges unipersonal managements. The
only legitimate authority in the Church must be that
of love and service, following the example of the Lord.

Such frank—if infelicitously translated—language speaks
loudly in the report. The cries of the ignored, marginalized, and
misunderstood color the report and the authors honestly record
them. The substantial section given over to "rethinking women's
participation" is illustrative of the centrality of women's multiple
roles in a Church that has yet to fully value their diverse contributions. The argument made over the years—and I heard it regularly at the '85 Extraordinary Synod—that women and ministry,
whether sacramental or otherwise, was a North American and
Western Europe ideological fixation and that the rest of the global

Church had no interest in the rarefied feminist theological advocacy that sought the full inclusion of women in the life and governance of the Church, is put to bed by this report. Women, across all the continents, whatever their culture, history, or formation, have a vested interest in the flourishing of the Church—and that flourishing needs to be enabled in both the particular and universal Church. At the same time, given the multiplicity of voices and perspectives, it should be no surprise that the report does not come to any kind of definitive summary or complete response to the question of the vocation, inclusion, and flourishing of women in Church and society. After careful listening, many consultation summaries ask that the Church continue its discernment in relation to a range of specific questions: the active role of women in the governing structures of Church bodies, the possibility for women with adequate training to preach in parish settings, and a female diaconate. A much greater diversity of opinion was expressed on the subject of priestly ordination for women, which some reports call for, while others consider it a closed issue. It remains a peculiarity of the discussion around women that in some fundamental way it is anomalous. Why should gender be a determinate of full inclusion? Why do we question women in/and the Church when men in/and the Church is a given? The deeper cultural-historical-anthropological dimensions of this discussion have yet to be fully explored. The biblical appears to be consigned to the margins, the ontological and canonical enjoying privileged priority, the ecumenical sidelined. There are many signs that Francis understands the stakes involved and that they are high. After all, in his position as Bishop of Rome he exercises the Petrine ministry of unity. But the fact remains that in the vast majority of the listening sessions and throughout all the written reports, issues around women and their mosaic of contributions calling for validation and institutionalization underscore the continent-wide priority of women in the Church.

The '85 Synod delegates, so quick to dismiss the "women's issue" as an evanescent phenomenon and an ideological product of a human-rights-obsessed feminist enclave of theologians that is in no way representative of women throughout the global Church, got it wrong.

The *Instrumentum Laboris of the 16th Ordinary Assembly of the Synod of Bishops—For a Synodal Church: Communion, Participation, Mission* is the official working document of the Synod on Synodality and consists of a skillful distillation of the ideas, recommendations, and proposals that surfaced during the period of extensive consultations and in the various reports that appeared during the diocesan and continental phases. It also provides direction for the synodal discussions, worksheets, and focus questions that constitute the majority of the time of the sessions. It recapitulates the heart of the synodal exercise itself when it states,

> The synodal assembly was asked to listen deeply to the situations in which the Church lives and carries out its mission. What it means to walk together when this question is asked in a particular context with real people and situations in mind.

A careful parsing of this passage from the *Instrumentum laboris* reveals the key concepts shoring up the synodal approach: listening deeply, walking together, with real people in mind.

Pope Francis has limited interest in self-referential ruminations and debates; he wants to address the anxieties and joys of humanity. Hence the release on October 4, 2023, of a second encyclical, *Laudate Deum* (Praise God), on the themes of environmental degradation, the throwaway mentality, the culture of abandonment, and care for our common home—timed for both the opening of the synod and for the feast day of St. Francis, his namesake and the guiding spirit of his papacy.

FROM FRANCIS TO FRANCISCO

Still, the synod is also about the internal life of the Catholic Church. Exhortations addressed to the world to attend with renewed passion and urgency the human justice and planetary issues without including the serious issues of injustice within the Church will compromise its credibility from the outset.

As one example, we have the cries for justice, penance, and reconciliation emerging from the Indigenous peoples of the earth. Cries that have been either misunderstood, neglected, or suppressed. Francis addressed their history of abuse in Bolivia in 2015 and in Canada in 2022.

As Archbishop Don Bolen of Regina, Saskatchewan, observed:

> The Synod is building on the Amazon Synod and the pope's visit to Canada with its emphasis on walking together. In both cases, the special gifts of Indigenous spirituality and culture were showcased....I am so grateful for Francis's leadership, for his humanity, his humility, his exceptional intelligence, his ability to speak wisely to so many parts; he has humanized the papacy; he has humanized church leadership...he is creating open spaces in a time of polarization; there is a transparency in his leadership and he admits his mistakes. He is teaching us a way of *being* church.[17]

Anticipating being on-site for the Synod on Synodality brings with it feelings of acute anticipation and fervent hopes, all tempered by the resurrection of memories of previous synodal moments with their aggravating defaults.

Will this Synod be a *bousculade*, a mad scramble, or will it be a *galimafrée*, a ragout of diverse morsels? It will be both. And that is its saving genius.

Francis is not averse to making a mess. In fact, he has encouraged Catholic youth to do precisely that, and he has spoken frequently of the image of the Church as a reverse pyramid, with the episcopacy, including the Bishop of Rome, at the bottom. Now that is a radical restructuring.

This Synod on Synodality was prefaced with a level of consultation beyond all previous consultations: surveys, questionnaires, diocesan reports, continental reports, academic conferences, elaborate data-gathering initiatives, massive media coverage, and, not surprisingly, resistance from some, a backlash from others, with arrestingly frank denunciations of Francis and his presumed efforts to reduce the Catholic Church to a liberal Protestant offshoot, a parliamentary assemblage, or a wildly equalitarian cult full to the brim with woke sentiments.

These are caricatures, calumnies really, and they will be exposed as such by the success of the synod itself: there will be no heretical proclamations, no sundering of the apostolic college, no schism-in-the-making, and no forsaking of the creative traditions of Catholic intellectual and spiritual life.

Rather, it will be a flowering of the Spirit and there will be healthy contestations of ideas, political lobbying (yes, the Vatican is not inured to political stratagems, as history can amply attest), some platforming and positioning as various groups make compelling arguments for their positions regarding justice issues, women and ministry, presbyteral reformation, the moral gravity of planetary peril due to depredations of the environment by centuries of human misrule, and other matters as well. A possible Pandora's box?

The alternative to risking a free and open discussion of ecclesial issues facing the Catholic communion is withdrawal, retreat, entombment. For Francis, such an option runs counter to the will of his Lord. This pope is fearless in heeding the gospel injunction to speak to all nations; he knows that Catholic tribalism runs counter to the expansionist vision of the evangelists, and he knows that the boundary lands are where we often encounter Jesus.

Francis is calling us to a pioneer Catholicism—an imaginative exploration of new territories of mind and spirit.

Will the synod sink under the weight of unrealistic expectations? Will it implode because of bureaucratic chaos and papal mismanagement? Or will it be the richest opportunity since the close of the Second Vatican Council to make sense of our Christian calling in a darkening landscape? For me, it will be both a *bousculade* and a *galimafrée*.

Let the synod begin.

II

THE FIRST SESSION

October 2023

SEPTEMBER 30, 2023–THE FEAST OF ST. JEROME

FLYING FROM TORONTO to Rome is not uncommon for me. Beginning in 1971, I have been to Rome over twenty-five times and in various capacities: pilgrim, tourist, researcher, administrator, and teacher. And so the memories are many, all contributing in some way to the Catholic mosaic of heart, mind, and spirit that makes up me. Here are a few from past Rome visits that I have dredged up, a stark reminder that Rome's hold on one is peculiar and perduring:

- A violent addict who resented my decision not to give him money followed me—releasing as he did a torrent of colorful expletives drawn creatively from numerous languages—into the sixteenth-century Chiesa Nuova, the New Church ("new" is relative in Rome), as I prudentially opted for Mass over an altercation. The church is known as the home of St. Philip Neri and is a powerhouse of preaching. Well, thank God, not this time. The church failed to deliver on its reputation. Though my accoster waited patiently in a back pew for Mass to end, and I sweated distractedly in a front pew occupied by my plans to elude him, by the time the presider got to the homily, he was gone. The sermon did him in.

- Cardinal Sebastiano Baggio was a major player in the world of Vatican politics—and beyond. On one occasion, while hosting me in his palatial digs, he highlighted the various artifacts, *objets d'art*, and other costly reminders of Vatican postings past. One Indigenous sculpture especially struck me. He mentioned that he was able to preserve it following a mob attack on the papal nunciature in Colombia. One of his *monsignori* held the mob at bay while the cardinal secured it. I asked what happened to the monsignor, and with a cursory wave of the hand implied he didn't quite know the cleric's plight or thought my inquiry discourteous.

- Attending, more by default than design, the annual mass of commemoration for the Swiss Guards slaughtered in defense of the pontiff during the Sack of Rome in 1527—all of them, actually—I was struck by the prominence accorded the Black Aristocracy, the nobility that remained loyal to the pope following the annexation of the Papal City States and Rome in 1870. They were dressed in black, of course, but no longer mourning the pope's lost real estate in this instance—rather, honoring the reverent memory of the guards massacred five centuries ago. Who am I to question their fealty or piety? But I was struck by their hauteur, their natural contempt for underlings like myself. There wasn't a Maggie Smith or Peter Ustinov among the lot of them.

- The last occasion I saw Pope John Paul II was when he was wheeled into the Sala Clementina on some moveable platform surrounded by carabinieri, security police, the customary ceremonial guard, the pure sound of a papal choir delivering a concert-level quality performance of "Tu es Petrus," and the pope's ever-watching and suspicious gatekeeper, Father Stanislaw Dziwisz (later created a cardinal). The pope was carted out to meet hundreds of presidents and rectors of Catholic universities, say a few words (given his stricken condition, words that were incomprehensible in any language), and nod favorably. Other than for a photo op, it struck me as unnecessary, and even unseemly, and not because of his infirmities—he bore them heroically—but because of the cult of personality so embedded in that papacy.

Popes stamp the city with their personality. Although it is a secular city and the capital of a different sovereignty, Rome and the Vatican for many people are interchangeable. Rome is where the pope hangs out and despite the Lateran Treaty that solved the Roman Question in 1929—establishing the Vatican City State and several extraterritorial entities as independent of Italy—the Roman landscape is quintessentially Catholic with its catacombs, holy ruins, basilicas, shrines, multiple educational institutions, and headquarters for countless religious orders and congregations. The Quirinal Palace is now one of the residences of the president of Italy when earlier it was a papal palace, and other shifts of ownership have occurred as well, most quite amicably—but Rome, Catholic Rome, remains the dominant reality in the city with its accredited international ambassadors, with its powerful ally—the Italian bishops conference and their own influential publications, and with its prestige as a conservator of culture (libraries, museums, choirs, paintings, and sculptures) without equal.

OCTOBER 1, 2023

A quick, prearranged limousine trip from Rome's Leonardo da Vinci–Fiumicino airport to my month-long accommodations with the Oblates of Mary Immaculate at their Generalate on the Via Aurelia. This was all due to the courtesy of one of the general councilors of the order, Raymond Mwangala, a Zambian Oblate I had taught at the Oblate School of Theology in San Antonio and whose doctoral dissertation on the spirituality of Henri Nouwen I directed. A dear friend, insightful scholar, and able administrator, Raymond embodies the gift of generosity.

Before bed I read "A Rat and Some Renovations" from the *Collected Stories* of Bernard MacLaverty, the Northern Irish writer, and laughed so heartily I couldn't get to sleep. A palliative for post-trip anxiety, for sure, but too potent in its capacity for body-shaking laughter to ease the soul and body into sleep.

OCTOBER 2, 2023

What a relief to actually get the badge that I must carry, religiously of course, to every event that allows the press access. Without the badge attesting to my official accreditation by the Press Office of the Holy See, I would simply be a roamer, a wanderer, without a base, without access, without network. Accreditation is good and necessary to have.

But the decision of the synod authorities—obviously with

Francis's support—to limit media access in order to ensure confidentiality around issues about which some speakers may hesitate to speak freely, does raise some concerns for me. I understand that there are costs to speaking freely, especially in an institution not hitherto known for its celebration of unhindered dialogue, and I appreciate the need for some serenity amidst a babble of words—but not all media types are mindless paparazzi driven by the next scandal or hungering for sensation.

We are a Church breathless with anticipation for a new way of speaking honestly and transparently. The Synod provides that way. To foreclose access, irrespective of the reasoning, sets off alarm bells for me. But this may be only the scars from my previous synod experiences speaking, with their tight control, redacted summaries, no access—never mind limited unsettling reminders of the past.

But my take on this is premature. Let's see how it plays out.

OCTOBER 3, 2023

There is a growing buzz around the *dubia*—those questions that arise out of doubt and seek doctrinal clarification—as, once again, Francis faces cardinalatial interrogation. In many ways, any prelate querying the pontiff on matters of doctrine and morals—and especially in a public forum—is historically unprecedented. Except in the Bergoglio papacy.

This is not his first go-around with these dissenting hierarchs. Following his post-synodal document *Amoris Laetitia*, four cardinals sought direction on concerns regarding divorced and remarried Catholics, the reception of communion by divorced Catholics, and other matters marital that especially exercise the legalistic mind, and Francis ignored them.

This time, on the cusp of the pope's Synod on Synodality, several of them have returned—with a few additions. The current round of dubia cardinals consists of two repeat interrogators: Raymond Burke, the U.S. bishop, canonist, and longtime Francis adversary who has held various positions in the Vatican including the Apostolic Signatura, the premier law court, and who has been jostled about with dismissals, reappointments, and reassignments, but no matter where he is remains the bur in the papal saddle; and the other repeat signatory is Germany's Walter Brandmüller, out of step big time with the vast majority of the German episcopate. The new signatories include Juan Sandoval of Mexico; former Vatican dicasterial prefect Robert Sarah, whose confrontational indiscretions on matters of liturgy and Church practice have earned papal rebukes; and Joseph Zen of Hong Kong, who has vigorously locked horns with Francis over the latter's efforts at rapprochement with China. Although Francis previously declined to be baited by the dubia, he has since accepted the risk and responded.

The questions—five in number—include the role of Divine Revelation, the widespread practice of blessing same-sex marriages, the nature of synodality as a "constitutive dimension of the Church," the sacramental ordination of women, and the discounting of repentance as a precondition for sacramental absolution.

In each instance the cardinals—all retired and no longer active—seek to pressure the pope to affirm traditional thinking by invoking the memory, theology, and magisterial writings of St. John Paul II. He is the lodestar of their thinking. He embodies the healthy, firm, and continuous tradition Francis imperils with, as they see it, his reckless leadership.

In his responses to the dubia, Francis deploys the writings of the very same pope his critics religiously invoke, with adroit Jesuit-tinged rhetorical skill and effective, nuanced reasoning. A perfect illustration of this is his considered reaction to the question of the ordination of women to the presbyterate:

When St. John Paul II taught that we must affirm "definitively" the impossibility of conferring priestly ordination on women, he was in no way denigrating women and giving supreme power to men. St. John Paul II also affirmed other things....He also stated that if the priestly function is "hierarchical," it should not be understood as a form of domination but "is totally ordered to the holiness of the members of Christ" (St. John Paul II, *Mulieris dignitatem*, 27). If this is not understood, and practical consequences are not drawn from these distinctions, it will be difficult to accept that the priesthood is reserved only for men, and we will not be able to recognize the rights of women or the need for them to participate in various ways in the leadership of the Church.

And here with the following paragraph is the kicker:

On the other hand, to be rigorous, let us recognize that a clear and authoritative doctrine on the exact nature of a "definitive statement" has not yet been fully developed. It is not a dogmatic definition, and yet it must be adhered to by all. No one can publicly contradict it and yet it can be a subject of study, as was the case of the validity of ordinations in the Anglican communion.

For Francis's critics this is a dramatic example of Jesuitical reasoning. The case is closed, but it is not really closed. We have an official position, to be adhered to and recognized for its binding quality, but at the same time we have been less than scholarly in making the kinds of theological distinctions essential in recognizing both the commanding power of traditional formulations and the openness necessary for new insights and appropriate refinements. It should be noted that the responses to the dubia appeared with consummate timing. Garry O'Sullivan, founder and editor of the Dublin-based *The Synodal Times*, observed in an interview with me on October 4—the day of the opening of the synod—that "the clowns who crafted and delivered the dubia handed Francis the ideal tool for re-charging the momentum of the Synod." Francis was helped in this by his new head of the Dicastery for the Doctrine of the Faith, the Argentine theologian Victor Manuel Fernández, created a cardinal just five days before the opening of the synod and an advocate for the "Francis Project." Although it is not quite what Francis had in mind in his response to the dubia cardinals on the matter of what constitutes "authoritative," the meditation on authority provided by English Dominican, spiritual writer, former Master General of the Dominican order, and Synod retreat giver Timothy Radcliffe in his pre-Synod retreat to all the delegates and official experts is refreshingly pertinent:

> Many lay people have been astonished during the preparation for this Synod to find that they are listened to for the first time. They doubted their own authority and asked: Can I really offer something? But it is not just the laity who lack authority. The whole church is afflicted by a crisis of authority. An Asian archbishop complained that he had no authority. He said that "the priests are all independent barons, who take no notice of me." Many priests too say that they lost all authority. The sexual abuse crisis has discredited us.

Lost authority can only be reclaimed through authenticity of presence, through open and not opaque recognition of institutional misdeeds, and through a creative engagement with prophetic witness—however this plays out in each one's unique context. And this is precisely what this Synod is about, with its emphasis on listening and encounter: the recovery of credible and life-giving authority.

Both immediately before and concurrent with the synod are various events arranged by advocacy groups keen on promoting a deeper understanding behind the struggle for women and sacramental ministry. A prayer vigil sponsored by Women's Ordination Conference, Women's Ordination Worldwide, Catholic Women's Council, and Catholic Network for Women's Equality was held on the penultimate evening before the opening of the synod at the Basilica di Santa Prassede—named after a Roman woman who cared for the bodies of martyrs in the second century. The basilica is Byzantine in its architecture and houses many mosaics of well-preserved antiquity.

I attended the prayer vigil held in one of the side chapels and listened to the many testimonies of women of all ages as they spoke with heartfelt conviction of the pain associated with not living their call to sacramental ministry, of being prevented from serving the Church fully because of their exclusion from orders. They are here in Rome to remind the synod delegates, the dicasterial prefects, and the pontiff that, in the words of Mary Ellen Chown of the Catholic Network for Women's Equality, "we should add to Pope Francis's 'without prayer there is no Synod' that without women, there is no church."

If it is true, as Timothy Radcliffe said at a press conference, "that a synod is like an orchestra, with different instruments having their own music. This is why the Jesuit tradition of discernment is so fruitful. Truth is not arrived at by majority vote, any or more than an orchestra or a football team is *led by voting!*"; it is not at the same time altogether satisfactory that the female musicians perceive their contribution to the orchestral performance as unequal to their male counterparts. We know that in the world of contemporary music women are utterly and irreversibly equal and that indeed the maestro could as easily be a *maestra*.

I will leave the football analogy to others more competent to speak on it.

It is a leitmotiv running through the preparatory documents, numerous interviews, and guidelines around delegate discussions that the synod is not a parliament nor is it governed by parliamentary rules and protocols. Fair game. But I detect a certain derision colored by fear when some speak of the Church as a nonparliamentary structure, concerned that issues will be brought forward, votes taken, tallies calculated, that could alter the nature of the Church, weaken Church doctrine, and diminish papal power. Consensus, genuine and transformative listening, and honest confrontation with the pastoral realities of people's lives do incorporate some aspects of parliamentary governance, and that is not a bad thing.

Although the testimony profiles provided by the women speakers were of a piece and convincing as pastoral pleas for justice and inclusion, their approach lacked theological heft, thereby diminishing their persuasive power for the unconvinced. Although, to be frank, those in the chapel with me—numbering around forty—were mostly women, many young, a few sympathetic male partners, and all supportive. Perhaps the larger crowd, live-streamed, would have had a more diverse composition, but it struck me as an exercise of preaching to the converted. It has yet to be translated to the synod hall; so much depends on the process.

Still, the telling question uttered by theology student Barb Cozee—Who can bless and who can be blessed?—was as pointedly direct as the Prayer for the Synodal Path was irenically earnest:

Cultivate in us a holy, healthy restlessness
on this synodal path.
Make us unafraid of prophetic decisions
that take us along unchartered territory.

OCTOBER 4, 2023

And so it begins with pageantry that can compete with the House of Windsor. The Opening Mass for the Synod in St. Peter's Piazza commenced with a hierarchy-privileged procession. No surprise here. Synodal delegates, lectors, priests, *monsignori*, masters of ceremony, majordomos, bishops, archbishops, eparchs and patriarchs, and cardinals dicasterial and recently created. The pope was already on the dais, settled into his wheelchair.

It was all grand theatre, a precious panoply, the choirs, the colors, the genuine universality. Rather hard to see Francis's "inverted pyramid" in all this—still, a masterly choreography of ritual and symbol, a big part of the tradition not to be obscured or minimized. But the optics speak volumes: This is a male affair.

The homily hit many of the high points of synodal preparation and expectation. Francis, while speaking of the *gaze of Jesus capable of seeing beyond…a gaze that blesses…a welcoming gaze*, reminded his listeners that the gaze of the Lord that blesses also invites us to be a Church that, "with a glad heart, contemplates God's action and discerns the present. And which, amidst the sometimes-agitated waves of our time, does not lose heart, does not seek ideological loopholes, does not barricade itself behind preconceived notions, does not give in to convenient solutions, does not let the world dictate its agenda." Once again, Francis raises the canard of worldly political processes as a seduction to be avoided. "Here [at the General Assembly of the Synod] we do not need a purely natural vision, made up of human strategies, political calculations, or ideological battles. We are not here to carry out a parliamentary meeting or a plan of reformation. We are here to walk together with the gaze of Jesus." But surely collisions of mind and spirit are the primary means for deepening our understanding of the truth. Dialogue that is substantive is electric; advocating for a position need not imply rigidity of heart and mind. The heated and sometimes vitriolic contests of the early Church Fathers over matters apostolical and christological, and the rigorous debates of the friars—Dominicans and Franciscans—at the time of the new university foundations of the West in the medieval period, it would seem to me, offer attractive templates Francis seems determined to not replicate in their purest form for an already polarized Church. A wise pastoral decision, no doubt, but too risk-averse for me.

The anxiety around imitating secular processes is understandable but overstated. Concerns around access to delegates, a seal of confidentiality imposed on participants, and long-term silence—no talking about content and dynamics of discussion groups or *circuli minores* up to and including the second session of the Synod on Synodality in October of 2024—have created some hostile media reaction. At the first press briefing a rattled Director of Communications sought to soothe an animated reporter who asked him why such censures are being implemented when they run counter to the very spirit of synodality as described in the official documents. Confusion reigned. In a conversation with one of the voting delegates I was told that Francis insisted that they *should* communicate with the press, but he also noted that there were a number of bishops especially skittish about open access and who disagreed with his approach.

Certainly there are clerics—and possibly laity as well—who view openness to the media as a sign of capitulation to the priorities of the world over that of the Church, but when you consider this backdrop of dissension set against the pope's own eagerness to address the world, we once again see the institutional antinomies at work.

Still, Francis plays it coyly by enjoining on the delegates the simple maxim of prudence and pastoral caution when he says that "a certain fasting from the public word" would be advisable.

Today, Francis issued *Laudate Deum* (Praise God), his apostolic exhortation to all the people of goodwill on the climate crisis. It is a follow-up to *Laudato Si'*, scheduled for world release on his feast day—St. Francis of Assisi—and driven by a heightened urgency around our deteriorating planet Earth. He notes at the very beginning of his text that the responses to the climate upheaval afflicting our common home since the publication eight years ago of *Laudato Si'* "have not been adequate, while the world in which we live is collapsing and may be nearing the breaking point."

To that end, he reiterates many of his earlier fears, strengthened in their intensity by the realities on the ground. He has done his homework:

- All of creation is integrated; our common home consists of all living companions: "Ocean waters have a thermal inertia, and centuries are needed to normalize their temperature and salinity, which affects the survival of many species. This is one of the many signs that the other creatures of this world have stopped being our companions along the way and have instead become our victims."

- A human ecology that serves as an alternative to the hegemonic technocratic paradigm: "A healthy ecology is the result of interaction between human beings and the environment, as occurs in the indigenous cultures and has occurred for centuries in different regions of the earth....The great present-day problem is that the technocratic paradigm has destroyed that healthy and harmonious relationship." (Note, the notion of the technocratic paradigm that Francis critiques is drawn from his study of the work of the towering Italian-German thinker Romano Guardini.)

- We have allowed vested powers and elites to profit while others languish because of our enslavement to a heartless and ruinous free-market capitalism. It continues to be regrettable that global crises are being squandered when they could be occasions to bring about beneficial changes. This is what happened in the 2007–2008 financial crisis and again in the COVID-19 crisis. For "the actual strategies developed worldwide in the wake of [those crises] fostered greater individualism, less integration and increased freedom for the truly powerful, who always find a way to escape unscathed" (Final document of the Special Assembly for the Pan-Amazonian Region [2019]).

- The papal social teaching around the principle of subsidiarity (first introduced in 1931 by Pope Pius XI and invoked and expanded upon by John XXIII, Paul VI, John Paul II, Benedict XVI, and now Francis) remains a foundation stone for an equitable society: "The current challenge is to reconfigure and recreate [multilateralism] taking into account the new world situation."

- Papa Bergoglio's vision of an integral ecology is profoundly Franciscan; the Umbrian friar's joy-infused celebration of the plenitude of creation defines and directs the pope's thinking about our common home: "'The universe unfolds in God, who fills it completely...there is mystical meaning to be found in a leaf, in a mountain trail, in a dewdrop, in a poor person's face.' The world sings of an infinite Love: how can we fail to care for it?"

Pope Francis champions the poor, pleads for creative responses—no matter how quantitatively insignificant they may seem in our own eyes—to waste reduction, excoriates governments for their failure of nerve, denounces wealthy barons of industry with their scant regard for anything other than the maximization of profits for their shareholders, and links justice, social equality, and a mite of mystical rapture.

Although there are many eco-theologians, scientists, and activists in the Catholic Church working in tandem with their like-minded secular counterparts, one figure that doesn't loom largely in universal awareness but should, given the timelines, relevance, and epic integration of his thinking, is the philosopher-visionary John Moriarty. An Irish mystic, Moriarty wrote in *Invoking Ireland: Ailiu Iath n-hErend* (2005) that "Christianity isn't only a morality that has its source in divine command....Christianity [is] the lived apprehension of unity in plurality out of which an ecumenical morality [can prosper]. Ecumenical not just among human beings of different persuasions and languages. Ecumenical across all boundaries, among all species living and extinct, among all worlds visible and invisible." And further: "Our soul isn't only in ourselves. It is in the tree we are felling, and in the seal pup we are clubbing to a bloody death. It follows that our world doesn't only environ us. It is in us, and we are in it. From this it further follows that all damage to the world is damage to ourselves and that all damage to ourselves is damage to the world." This isn't simply a hybrid Franciscanism, an anti-Catholic pantheism indifferent to ontology. It is a Christo-cosmology in keeping with Bergoglio's vision for an integral ecology.

On the personal front: The intense and uncommon heat in Rome serves as a potent reminder of climate change even here in the Eternal City. Hot, hot, and hotter.

OCTOBER 5, 2023

The methodology employed by the synod authorities is painstakingly thorough, optimistic, and rather procrustean. The *circuli minores* consist of a dozen people per round table. These folk are representative of the continents, drawing on a wide variety of cultural and ethnic experiences, ensuring both youth and women are, if not showcased, clearly valued and present. The emphasis is on creating and sustaining a fraternal (pardon the semantic exclusivity) experience, journeying together with the Holy Spirit as the synod's protagonist. This kind of discourse smacks of pious piffle, but it does all the same speak to the underlying truths of the synod: a pilgrim people quickening their faith through a shared search for deeper communion. A search that is an encounter with the other; a search propelled by prayer and silence; a search attentive to the struggles of the alienated; a search defined by listening and compassion and not by declamation and judgment; a search open to renewal and even reform.

In a nutshell, this is how it works:

- The working groups, or small circles (*circuli minores*), are composed of a dozen representatives (voting delegates) in addition to a facilitator, a secretary, and a rapporteur. Continent origin, age, gender, and background experience, in addition to language facility, are key determinants in deciding on the composition of representatives.
- They have a worksheet that provides them with the question for discernment, the results of which are summarized in a written report of two pages.
- The report must be sensitive to points both of convergence and divergence.
- A three-minute intervention will be presented to the general congregation.
- The report and the intervention must recognize the consensus reached, acknowledging any divergences; they must also be approved by an absolute majority of the working group attesting to their faithful recording of the discussion (questions, proposals, and so forth).
- The plenary assembly allows for wider discussion among all working groups.
- Moments of silence will punctuate the process.
- The general congregations receive and listen to the contributions of the working groups but also

enable them to reread and modify their conclusions in light of the many perspectives emerging from the plenary assembly debates.

The structure of the synod with its round tables in the aula of the Paul VI Hall, with its almost draconian adherence to rules of engagement (interventions timed and number of pages fixed), with its intentional composition of the working groups ensuring variety of background and perspective, with its accompanying experts appointed by the General Secretariat to provide assistance, professional crafting services, and continuity of timely delivery, are admirable in their way. After all, how to guarantee maximum involvement of a large, disparate body gathered to share, illuminate, and discover if there isn't a tight methodology?

But I can't help but feel uneasy about a methodology that is reminiscent of the worst features of professional mission statements and industry-inspired strategic planning sessions, and studiously reliant on infuriatingly bland discourse.

The proof will be in the pudding.

OCTOBER 6, 2023

The diligent and tenacious reporter from England's *The Catholic Herald*, the conservative if not fundamentalist Diane Montagna, delights in prodding and probing the increasingly rattled Paolo Ruffini, prefect of the Dicastery for Communication. Or at least, rattled when she asked *her* questions. At today's press briefing she inquired why the synod authorities speak loudly and constantly about the Holy Spirit being the true Protagonist of the synod when the Holy Spirit's presence is best ascertained through Divine Revelation, the apostolic tradition, and the Magisterium. Perhaps, she mused, it is not the right Spirit guiding the synod. How can we be sure?

Ruffini's response was splintered and grasping and delivered in such animated Italian that I missed most of it. I will need to check this out.

OCTOBER 7, 2023

Such sweet excitement today. Finally, some fire in the press room. But before the fire there was a tepid report by Ruffini on the discussion around seminaries and priestly formation, culminating with a rejection of all forms of clericalism, including that which infects the laity. Clericalism, priestly training, and the continuing aftershocks of the yet-to-end sexual abuse crisis need to be addressed in such a way to reconceive formation and accommodate new ways of understanding the presbyterate. Concerns around declining seminary enrollments, and indeed closures of seminaries themselves—particularly in the West—are often mitigated by the growth in seminarians and in the building of new seminaries to house them in other jurisdictions. But this quantitative approach obscures the qualitative one: How do we make priestly ministry work in our time? The seminary is increasingly an institution of residual relevance only. Other models of formation need to be advanced, including non-stipendary assignments congruent with a professional working career. Also, a revival of the tragically aborted Worker-Priest Movement makes increasing sense in a Church plagued by unused and costly buildings along with the collapse of the traditional parish structure. And we haven't even alighted on women and ministry, the key to a flourishing and credible presbyterate of the future in a global Church. The Pontifical Commission for the Protection of Minors (a creation of Pope Francis that has been both successful and yet fraught with mission and personnel difficulties) issued a blistering reproach of the Church's inadequate response to the global problem of sexual abuse on the eve of the synod. But not a despairing one. The commission reminded the synod delegates that

> the reality of sexual abuse in our Church goes to the heart of the Synod's agenda. It deals with who we are as a community of faith, founded on Jesus. It permeates discussions on leadership models, ministry roles, professional standards of behavior, and of being in right relationship with one another and all of creation....We urge you to dedicate meaningful time and space to integrate the testimony of victim/survivors into your work....We urge you to work towards the day when our Church takes full account and full responsibility for the wrongs done to so many in its care.... We urge you to work towards the day when transparent and accessible systems of wrongdoing by the Church's minsters function well according to acceptable standards....We urge you to work towards these long-overdue goals not for just one or two days during your gathering, but to consider them throughout the entire Synod process.

At the same time that the commission letter was released, a flood of new scandals in Australia, Switzerland, and France highlighted the enduring failure of the Church to firmly and definitively deal with this moral Medusa. It is the sex abuse scandals in Germany that prompted their bishops to take a radical approach to structural and doctrinal reform through their own national synod, thereby prompting alarm among many members of the global episcopate—some of whom signed a letter to their German counterparts expressing alarm at the potential for schism. The Vatican entered the fray, cautioned the Germans to temper expectations and not get ahead of the global process, and even resulted in a few logistic adjustments, such as having the German delegates not hived off into their own linguistic small circles but compelled to pick one of the other language groups.

But today! Today the customary Stampa personnel were accompanied by two livewires: Sister Leticia Salazar of the Company of Mary Our Lady, Chancellor of the Diocese of San Bernardino, California, and Cardinal Fridolin Ambongo Besungu, a Capuchin, archbishop of Kinshasa, Democratic Republic of the Congo, and president of the Symposium of Episcopal Conferences of Africa and Madagascar.

The fiery nun from California spoke of the "deep experience of the globality of the church" and was especially pointed in her concern over migration issues—a global, not regional, concern. The cardinal coyly observed that although he attended previous synods, this synod is unlike any other in that previously "we knew what the outcomes and proposals were before we even started and this time there is no agenda; we are *living* this synod with confidence and joy."

The cardinal's frankness—a not-so-subtle dig at the top-down managerial control of synods of the previous popes, John Paul II in particular—seems to have particularly irked the conservative Catholic and secular press.

Le Figaro, the avowedly right-wing French daily, was first to strike. "What makes this synod authoritative in terms of understanding and interpreting the will of God and why is it special in this regard? Is it any more authoritative than any other gathering of bishops at either a synod or council"?

The cardinal spoke of authority originating in the common priesthood of all believers sealed by our baptism, as revealed through our attentive listening to the will of God in the movements of the Spirit.

As was the case with the *Catholic Herald* yesterday, every effort is being made by conservatives to undermine the special status of the Synod on Synodality by underscoring its seeming indifference to doctrinal clarity and magisterial integrity by means of a vocabulary so fluid, so averse to traditional categories of expression, and so porous in its definitions that we have nothing more than a muddle. Francis's "make a mess" is unfolding before our very eyes.

A further rejection of the synodal approach came from the *National Catholic Register* when its reporter boldly challenged the cardinal—and all his conservative interrogators, I should note, have been obsequiously polite with a special fondness for honorifics belying their true intent—when he asked how an African prelate would respond to the push for LGBTQ+ acceptance by the Magisterium when his own continent has made clear what it thinks of homosexuality.

The cardinal responded by saying that synodality is a journeying *together*, that we are not finished in our task of understanding and making operative a truly synodal Church, and that the reporter should ask for his opinion at the conclusion of the second session of the synod next year.

His Solomonic response has bought him some time.

OCTOBER 8, 2023

Respite, reprieve, and reenergizing. A day off and time to explore Trastevere, a venerable and crowded area of Rome long associated in the Catholic and ecumenical world with the Sant'Egidio Community—an ecclesial lay movement committed to peacemaking, social justice for the poor, and the deep integration of prayer with action. Its founder, Andrea Riccardi, is a historian and a one-time cabinet minister responsible for international cooperation and integration policies for the government of Mario Monti. Riccardi's *To the Margins: Pope Francis and the Mission of the Church* (originally published in Italian in 2016) highlights marginality as the magna carta of the Bergoglio papacy.

OCTOBER 9, 2023

Bit of a flurry as the press office provided access by monitor to the Paul VI aula, where the discussion groups busily listened, prayed, and discussed—with us as detached observers. Not the most riveting cinema. After all, the interpersonal dynamic is the key to unlocking the mysteries and muddles of the synodal process.

Pranzo (the Italian leisurely big meal of the day) with the Vatican correspondent for London's *The Tablet* (shortly to begin a new journalist venture with CNN)—the articulate, youthful, and insightful Christopher Lamb—proved a much more satisfactory exercise in human encounter than a stationary role virtually watching an earnest audience at a distance.

Lamb agrees with fellow Englishman Radcliffe's understanding of what synodality requires of us: passionate love. The Dominican friar's spiritual input this morning, as the delegates begin week two, was centered on Jesus and the Samaritan woman and underscores the nature of that passionate love. The erudite Radcliffe, with a predilection for literary bon mots admixed with sporadic snippets of whimsy, begins his definition of passionate love by invoking the leader of a rival religious order, the Basque Pedro Arrupe of the Society of Jesus:

> Our formation for synodality means learning to become passionate people, filled with deep desire. Arrupe, the marvelous superior general of the Jesuits, wrote: "Nothing is more practical than finding God, that is, than falling in love in a quite absolute, final way. What you are in love with, what seizes your imagination, will affect everything....Fall in love, stay in love, and it will decide everything."

As Radcliffe further states,

> A synodal church will be one in which we are formed
> for unpossessive love: a love that is neither abusive
> or cold....We should be formed for deeply personal
> encounters with each other, in which we transcend
> easy labels. Love is personal and hatred is abstract.
> [Let me] quote from Graham Greene's novel *The Power
> and the Glory*, "Hate was just a failure of imagination."

Lamb shares Radcliffe's conviction that the synod is a different way of living as Church, but he has a more realpolitik
approach to the internal forces aligned against Francis: "It has
been said by some that Francis appears to be the *only* person at
the synod that the Spirit is *not* working through. The synod is
open-ended and risky and we don't know how to work it out yet.
Francis's critics see that as his weakness. But as a Jesuit he sees
it as his strength."[1]

OCTOBER 10, 2023

It was surprising to hear from both the liberal Catholic
press and their conservative equivalents at today's press briefing
that there doesn't appear to be much time for honest exchange of
opinion among the delegates. This struck today's presiding prelate and guest—the ever-amiable and adroit Joseph Tobin, cardinal archbishop of Newark, New Jersey, and a staunch Francis
ally—to respond incredulously that

> I have attended seven synods—five as Superior-
> General of the Congregation of the Most Holy Redeemer

(the Redemptorists) and two as a bishop—and the Synod on Synodality is the most diverse synod I have ever attended. At past synods the bishops would say that we can't talk about what we want to talk about. Differences of opinion under the new rubric are not seen as divisive but as complementary. Throughout the entire synodal process—and I have been involved from the beginning—preparatory, diocesan, continental and now at the synod proper—the level of consultation has been unprecedented. Laity and clergy said what they thought and trusted that it would be faithfully recorded—not necessarily the emphasis they attached to it but certainly the content. As an example of how the laity who participated in my archdiocese felt connected and affirmed let me quote one of my auxiliary bishops. Manuel Aurelio Cruz—affectionately called Manny—is Cuban born with a taste for the artistic. He has spoken about the arresting beauty of our cathedral, which he says is the most beautiful in North America, but it is *most* beautiful when the doors are open. A perfect metaphor for this synod.

This strikes me as a slightly extravagant claim, considering some of the cathedrals and basilicas dotting the Mexican and Canadian landscape. But who am I to quibble with such an ardent declaration by an auxiliary bishop?

Tobin especially insisted on seeing the evolution of the synod process from its static existence—*Lineamenta*, *Instrumentum laboris*, various propositions/proposals, post-synod papal document—to its new dynamic existence with detailed pre-synod consultations and documents, fully engaged discussion circles, and no predetermined outcomes, as most welcome.

OCTOBER 11, 2023

Today's press briefing highlight was the primate of the Church in Canada, Cardinal Gérald Lacroix, archbishop of Quebec City, and a member of the Ordinary Council of the Synod. A former missionary to Latin America and a respected prelate in Canada as well as in the Vatican, Lacroix provided some opening reflections that were essentially an essay or extended homily. Part theological analysis, part pastoral exhortation, and part personal testimony to the power of transformation, the synod's Second Vatican Council pedigree and its ecumenical dimension are constitutive of its mission and success. A bit of a windy expostulation by comparison to previous speakers, but substantive.

Although the synod is an enclave unto itself, sealed off from intruders, paparazzi, nosey tourists, and importunate pilgrims, it is not sealed off from the world. How could it be *this* Synod if it were! The continuing nightmare that is Ukraine's struggle for existence and now the savagery unleashed in Israel and Gaza draw the delegates into a centered world of prayer, silence, and reflection. It is not the first time in Rome's storied history that it has been besieged by the hordes of horror—literal and metaphorical.

OCTOBER 12, 2023

Colazione (breakfast) with Chris White, indefatigable Vatican correspondent of the *National Catholic Reporter*, was refreshingly informative. White has covered all the Bergoglio synods to date, and I have only covered several of Wojtyla's, so I was especially interested to get his take on the way this synod is unfolding:

In past synods delegates were free to speak at will because they were more scripted and as a consequence, they gave talks, published pieces, met with journalists, and talked outside the confines of the structured meetings. They published their own interventions after delivering them. They helped shape the conversation in the room because they were in the room even while speaking out of it. Now they are fearful of speaking because the pope sees this synod as a spiritual retreat and not as a personality-driven event. But many of us, journalists as well as the lay folk back home we report for, find this very frustrating because of the tone and expectations set by the pope over the last two years of preparatory work.[2]

White's point is well taken and speaks to the ambivalence many of us feel toward the position taken by Francis. I certainly appreciate his intention to eliminate the pressures on the delegates to perform for their audience, to insist that the synod is a spiritual event that must incorporate elements of silence, prayer, and reverence for the other. And, for sure, many feel that their freedom to speak will be compromised by media interviews, public perceptions, and potential polarities of view that can shatter the peace and trust they have built up as a community of discernment.

But the downside is considerable and arguably detrimental to the synod itself. The progressive or liberal media find themselves in a strange place. Widely sympathetic to Francis and his spirit of openness, we now find ourselves constrained in what we can do. All that we can rely on, publicly at least, are the anodyne commentaries and summaries provided by the press office, while our traditionalist or conservative colleagues are free to critique without limit what they see as a Francis-generated cabal hell-bent on changing the Church itself.

Without reliable information that speaks to the conversations actually going on in the aula, without a concrete sense of the interpersonal dynamics at the small circles, without any real apprehension of the dissonances at the table, the liberal camp is reduced to complaining and wearing down their sources. The conservatives, on the other hand, see the paucity of data as yet another instance of the secret agenda of this pontificate.

Today the synod office announced the election of—and papal appointments to—the Commission for the Synthesis Report and the Commission for Information. The membership of both commissions is top-heavy with prelates, ex officio supernumeraries, and Vatican apparatchiks and so unwieldy as to be a formidable operational challenge. Still, the genuinely universal makeup of these two bodies speaks once again to the globality of the synod. I am not interested in adding yet another neologism to the current vocabulary but the term *globality* strikes me as appropriate shorthand in the way that catholicity came to describe essential Catholic self-definition by institutions linked to Catholicism around the time of the publication in 1990 of the Vatican document on Catholic higher education, *Ex Corde Ecclesiae* (From the Heart of the Church).

And the presence of Sister Pat Murray of the Institute of the Blessed Virgin Mary (Loretto Sisters) on the Synthesis Commission is an especially sapiential choice.

OCTOBER 13–14, 2023

Running parallel with the synod within the walls (the Paul VI Hall delegates) is the lay-led Synodal Assembly beyond the walls (the Domus Bonum Pastor conferees). The latter group does not constitute an official Vatican entity; quite the contrary. Supported by numerous lay-sponsored bodies throughout the Church—We are Church, Root & Branch, Catholic Network for Women's Equality, Women's Ordination Conference, Future Church, Concerned Lay Catholics in Canada, and many more besides—the assembly, both virtual and on-site, is the brainchild of Spirit Unbounded, and the specific focus of the two-day counter-synod is on human rights in the emerging Catholic Church. There have been other events and celebrations and protests and encounters prior to this weekend summit but this gathering is the culmination. And it is not counter in the sense that it is designed to negate the work of the Roman Synod, but rather the planners see it as a positive and critical companion along the synodal way. More advocacy than exchange in its emphasis, this assembly provides an opportunity for focused attention punctuated with personal appeals for justice from a Church that remains *semper reformanda* (ever-reforming).

I thought I should attend.

And I am glad that I did.

The two-day synodal assembly—live-streamed from both Rome and Bristol—was designed from the outset as lay-dominant and although avowedly non-adversarial in its approach and tone, it was often blistering in its criticism. Paola Lazzarini Orrù—a sociologist, founder of Donne per la Chiesa (Women for the Church), as well as a journalist—launched a broadside against the Church's restrictive and often hypocritical clerical lordship. She sardonically observed in her opening remarks that a perfect illustration of the inequity experienced by women in Italy, in even the most educated of quarters, can be seen in the strange concatenation of circumstances wherein writers for the respected and authoritative Jesuit journal, *La Civiltà Cattolica*, can be found writing about the spiritual abuse of women upstairs while in the basement the women are doing the laundry and preparing the meals.

Ouch.

And that was certainly not the snarkiest comment of the day. I think it is important to allow for such moments of frustration, anger, and disappointment, for after all, although the "conversations in the Spirit" characteristic of the official synod may be revolutionary in the Vatican sphere and a new mode of engagement, "conversations of pain" in the activist sphere have long been the defining modality. Although the synod delegates are religiously adhering to the papal admonition that they not serve as conduits of information to the media, thereby shattering the cone of trust and honesty, stuff still leaks. No convocation of such magnitude can possibly seal all talk from getting out. Social media provides a platform for individual griping even when it appears to be neutral and semi-anonymous. For instance, in the last four days we have heard that an Eastern Rite patriarch berated the Jesuit priest and writer Jim Martin, taking his bottle of water and with high moral dudgeon moving to another table; the retired dicasterial cardinal and former head of the body that recommends the appointment of bishops, Marc Ouellet, departed in a huff visibly frustrated by the synodal process; the media celebrity bishop Robert Barron has manifested a certain grumpiness and dissatisfaction other delegates have picked up on—perhaps nastily assigning his change of mood to his media blackout. Gossip, possibly? Incomplete data, very likely. People want information, and when they don't get it, the vacuum is filled with speculation, lots of unhelpful murmuration, the juicy bits, and a dollop or two of fanciful invention.

The Synodal Assembly presentations were of diverse format and content: historical, ethical (also including syntheses and critiques of classical moral theology in relation to natural law), biblical and patristic, personal and communal, spiritual, liturgical, and polemical.

Special highlights consisted of presentations by two feminist warhorses—the redoubtable Benedictine Joan Chittister and the insuppressible lawyer Mary McAleese. They not only provided discrete offerings, but they also ran a panel of two with their wit, erudition, and sporadic outrage—righteous, of course—ensuring plenty of crowd-pleasers delivered with both high-powered rhetoric and personal warmth.

Performance art.

Although I had a stimulating conversation with McAleese and have read her and listened to her in the past, we had not met before. Chittister I have known for years, dating back to a major conference on women in the Church in Washington. Subsequently, I interviewed her for my CBC Radio One *IDEAS* series, *Monasticism as Rebellion*, invited her to St. Jerome's University in Waterloo as part of the Centre for Catholic Experience Lectures Series, and appointed her as a contributing editor of *Grail: An Ecumenical Journal*, a publication I edited for a dozen years. It was marvelous to reconnect after an absence of two decades.

Chittister and McAleese know how to push the right buttons. Both are skilled in the rhetorical arts—in fact, Chittister has a doctorate in rhetoric—and both know that their effectiveness as speakers relies on a clever mélange of exhortatory prose with a whiff of the oracular, spiced with humor both gentle and acidic, direct eye contact coupled with glancing references to a printed text, and an ability to connect with their audience via the heart as well as the head.

Their presentations as well as their panel repartee spoke to passion *through* passion, and although they drew from a well of jokes and narratives that were variously tired, refreshing, modestly incendiary, open to a historical reductionism for maximum effect, and all richly seasoned by their sincerity, they resuscitated debates of the past with a new prophetic urgency. They sensed that their presence in Rome this time had intimations of *Kairos*.

OCTOBER 16, 2023

I assumed before I arrived in Rome this time that writing a book on the Synod on Synodality—the Francis project par excellence—was going to be a piece of cake. After all, he has changed the very makeup and operation of the synod itself: expanded membership including laywomen and men with the right to vote; a two-year preparation including the most extensive consultation prior to a Vatican event on record; an astonishing degree of openness regarding process and procedure, the much-vaunted *parrhesia*; a breadth of composition hitherto unheard of. In other words, a joy to witness, record, and analyze.

And then Francis dropped that bombshell practically on the eve of the synod's opening: There is to be custody of the tongue, a "fasting of the word," with delegates instructed not to give interviews to the media or provide parallel commentaries on the proceedings in the Paul VI aula. The reasons for such an unprecedented restriction are grounded in the pope's convictions that: synodality needs to be experienced in an atmosphere of mutual trust; participants must feel free to share in an environment enveloped in prayer that respects their own vulnerabilities; "conversations in the Spirit" will be compromised if there is a steady flow to the microphones and the scribblers; and that the primary purpose of collective discernment is threatened by fanciful speculation, willful invention, and the toxin of gossip.

I have further thoughts on the matter. First, Francis has a point. This synod assembly is as much a spiritual undertaking as an intellectual one and if this can only be secured within a shroud of secrecy or constricting discretion, so be it. But there is a price to pay, a price Francis may have decided was worth it or a price whose exacting cost he hadn't anticipated.

When you foreclose the transmission of information and curtail contacts by insisting on nondisclosure of discussion content, you don't create a healthy relationship with the media. And remember, this is a pope who loves a scrum with journalists, delights in the occasional kibbitz, and has publicly valued the importance of the media to the Church with their morally necessary investigative work.

At past synods I covered, the Vatican's director of communications or media was the Opus Dei layman Dr. Joaquín Navarro-Valls and subsequently the Italian Jesuit, Federico Lombardi—and they both presided with professional gravitas, even if sometimes flustered by occasional bureaucratic inefficiencies. By contrast, the current team is often a version of the Keystone Cops, easily rattled, fearful, and running about in all directions. After the press room was vacated following today's briefing, I asked an assistant if I could use one of the empty rooms for a brief fifteen-minute interview with a young doctoral student at the Graduate Theological Union in Berkeley whose work will center on synodality. I was told that my request was reasonable but that it had to go to his superior. She, in turn, found the request not out of order but she needed to secure the permission of her superior. At this rate, it seemed to me, my request could end up on the desk of the Roman Pontiff. But no, a surly factotum came to see me and said that it was out of the question, and I would have to conduct the interview on the street. Astonishing. I suggested in a rather animated way that a press office is conventionally designed to enable the press to do their work and not to erect obstacles for them. He was unpersuaded and dismissive.

This incident followed immediately after I sought out, in one of the press antechambers, the sharp and affable Sister Pat Murray (appointed to the Synthesis Commission charged with drafting the Final Report) to bring her greetings from the Institute of the Blessed Virgin Mary (Loretto Sisters) in Toronto as well as from friends in Thornbury, Ontario. I had to do this with dispatch as I feared being tasered by her scowling minder.

This is not an ideal working relationship. It has soured many in the profession. We want a scrum-friendly Francis back, and quick.

It would have been better to set aside the first week or two, following Timothy Radcliffe's imaginative and inspiring retreat meditations, to initiate the delegates into the new synodal way of doing things—ensuring the buy-in spiritually and intellectually—and then to move to a different modality outside the aula allowing for forthright engagement with the media.

The Catholic world has invested so much in this synod, they

need to hear the good news—and from what has surreptitiously leaked, there is lots of good news.

OCTOBER 17, 2023

Yesterday the issue of women in ministry appears to have led to a level of high animation, with all topics raised apropos of the role of women in the Church on the table and all done in a climate of shared respect and openness. But at the press briefing today the theologian Renée Köhler-Ryan of Notre Dame University, Australia, in response to a question inquiring about the status of women in ordained ministries—diaconate and presbyterate—downplayed the issue, minimized it really, by speaking personally about women and the professions, the multiple roles women currently have in Church governance and service, and the simple fact that she has never wanted to be a priest and thinks the discussion emphasis is disproportionate.

She could have benefitted from the lay-assembly debates if for no other reason than to see that for many women who sincerely believe, as St. Thérèse de Lisieux did, that they are called to the priesthood, the question of women and ordained ministry is not a private obsession, a matter for single-issue advocacy, or a niche concern. Rather snide and dismissive to reduce it to such easy caricaturing, although Köhler-Ryan did make some solid points around the diversity of women's voices in the *circuli minores*, reminding everyone that the presence of mothers and fathers, heard for the first time in a synod of the universal Church, is a great gift.

The Nigerian Jesuit theologian Agbonkhianmeghe Orobator has a penchant for the essential summary and neatly outlined the synodality experience by situating it in both a personal and communal context. I must confess that Orabator's impressive synthesizing abilities overrode what I took to be a mannered, if not precious, mode of oral delivery. Clearly, however, his sooth-ing and unrufflable style was a palliative for some of the more edgy commentary in evidence at the briefing. This is a privileged moment for a theologian to be on the ground of a Church making and remaking itself. The synod really begins when it ends: when convergence and consensus, divergence and difference combine into a new and creative constellation, synodality comes alive.

A feisty and veteran Vatican commentator and reporter, Cindy Wooden, took on Communications Dicastery head Paolo Ruffini today, reprimanding him for dismissing questions as merely journalistic as if the issues around women and LGBTQ+ were of peripheral concern. I have never come across someone in charge of communications who seems to have such a low opinion of journalists. It may be his limited command of languages, or it may be an impatient temperament, but whatever the explana-tion, time for a performance review.

Wooden received vigorous applause. She spoke for every sentient journalist in the room.

OCTOBER 18, 2023

Once again today the conservative faction raises the issue of homosexuality, an issue they obsess about with distressing tenacity. They regularly raise the 1986 document, *Letter to the Bishops of the Catholic Church on the Pastoral Care of Homosexual Persons*, which was issued by the Congregation for the Doctrine of the Faith. This document, they argue, is authoritative, defini-tive, and unnuanced. They also fear change on the horizon. And so reporters from *Life-Site News*, *The Catholic Herald*, *National Catholic Register*, and others of similar disposition push for a reaffirmation of that document's teaching, for clarity on matters of Divine Revelation, for a strengthening of magisterial authority in a time of unprecedented slippage.

They don't get the answers they want—but neither does the progressive press. We are told that the process is primary, cultural sensitivity is a priority, and honest exchanges of opinion are protected from outside scrutiny.

But symbols work, and optics count. During the same week that a Latvian bishop tied himself into knots of opacity trying to distinguish Catholic teaching from pastoral practice, a bishop from Oceania disapproved of the Western habit of labeling everyone and opted for the use of a Filipino word for all humans irrespective of gender, a nineteen-year-old from Wyoming warbled on agreeably regarding synodal process, and the Holy Father, the pope, met with Sister Jeannine Gramick. Gramick is the pioneer advocate for LGBTQ+ issues in the Catholic Church who has experienced calumny and suppression from previous high-ranking prelates but who has formed a relationship with Francis, principally by correspondence and now in the flesh, that is bearing fruit. Her meeting with him, accompanied by three members of New Ways Ministry, cannot avoid inflaming the pope's critics, persuaded as they are of a hidden agenda, an openness to reform, and a determination to usurp Church teaching.

The conservative press is having all the fun; the progressives have only snippets and shards.

OCTOBER 19, 2023

Today's briefing was on migration and the panel of guest experts/synod delegates were closely familiar with the geopolitical and economic ruination incurred by populace displacement, rampant homelessness, and despair as a consequence of uprooting, and the pastoral challenges that beset migrants at every level: familial, emotional, fiscal, and health-wise.

Cardinal Michael Czerny, the Czech-Canadian Jesuit who is the prefect for the Dicastery for Promoting Integral Human Development, was the critical go-to person on the panel.

Given the considerable influence he sways as a prefect, his sturdy Jesuit credentials, his extensive exposure to Central American upheaval and African carnage, and his special proximity to Francis, we need to know more, much more, about this *éminence rouge et grise*.

Czerny's presence on today's panel allowed him to speak to the contrast between the security, privilege, and order of the synod delegates with their lives and that of the homeless migrants with their vulnerability, marginalization, and chaos.

In this he was in strong alignment with Daniel Flores, bishop of Brownsville, Texas—a border diocese at the very geographical heart of migrant turmoil and suffering—when the latter spoke movingly of conversion of the heart. Flores noted that the synodal dynamic is a "translation" of cultures and attitudes and that in respectful talking and listening we are living synodality outside the aula and on the streets.

OCTOBER 20, 2023

Mary Theresa Barron, the Irish president of the International Union of Superiors General, reminded everyone present at today's briefing that nuns have been living synodally for centuries and that their witness is a gift to the universal Church.

First Pat Murray, and now Mary Theresa Barron. What accounts for the Hibernian power couple? It is as if the vacuum created by a diminishing episcopal presence of solid leadership in the Irish Church has been replaced by two Irish nuns at the seat of Roman power.

Of special note with the bishops at the table today—Tarciso Isao Kikuchi, SVD, of Tokyo and Gintaras Grušas, president of the Bishops' Conferences of Europe—was a reminder again of the impressive universality of the Church. Grušas, for instance, is actually an American-Lithuanian, a mathematics graduate from

UCLA, and a spokesperson for forty-five European countries. Kikuchi is of the Divine Word Missionaries, who have a strong presence in Japan as I discovered when I attended an International Federation of Catholic Universities 2006 board meeting at the University of Nanzan in Nagoya. A year later I was hosting a senior official from the Japanese Embassy in Ottawa in my capacity as president of St. Thomas University in Fredericton, New Brunswick. I remarked on how impressed I was by the University of Nanzan—its range of offerings, its interfaith sensitivity, its well-earned reputation—and noted its German provenance. The official was outraged and said there were NO German-associated universities in Japan. I gently persisted that there certainly was one. "NO," thundered the apoplectic official, at which point my dean of humanities whispered in my ear: "Perhaps, boss, best to drop this topic as any memories of the Axis Powers Alliance can't be good for us." I dropped the topic.

Here at the synod, Kikuchi struck an interesting note that many of us missed: The Japanese, indeed many Asians, he insisted, love silence. They don't naturally speak up in a group setting so the *circuli minores* provided a safe environment in which to do so. The use of silence and prayer punctuating the discussions was an inviting feature of the Bergoglio synodal reinvention.

Both bishops spoke of how they will bring their experience of synodality to their dioceses and episcopal conferences, inviting all to "take off their shoes and come into my home to dialogue and speak honestly."

That's the goal; that's what the big tent is all about.

OCTOBER 21, 2023

Earlier in the week, the General Rapporteur, Cardinal Hollerich, identified in very clear terms the public credibility of the synod when he said,

We are all well aware that this Synod will be evaluated on the basis of the perceivable changes that will result from it. The big media, especially those farthest away from the Church, are interested in possible changes on a very limited number of subjects....But even the people closest to us, our collaborators, members of pastoral councils, people who are involved in parishes are wondering what will change for them, how they will be able to concretely experience in their lives that missionary discipleship and co-responsibility on which we have reflected in our work. And they are wondering how this is possible in a Church that is still not very synodal, where they feel that their opinion does not count and a few or just one person decides everything.

And this is where a strategy of credible, transparent, and efficient communication comes to play a central role.

In his spiritual input for the last week of the synod, Radcliffe rightly names the strange, quixotic, and yet alluring nature of acting synodally when he says, "The synodal process is organic and ecological rather than competitive. It is more like planting a tree than winning a battle, and as such will be hard for many to understand, sometimes including ourselves!"

Radcliffe, in his gentle way, admonishes the delegates to abjure the "party-political way of thinking [with its] sterile, barren language of much of our society." Irenic, for sure. And we have all tasted the savage polarizing inherent in irresponsible discourse, the flourishing of those who bank on graphic headlines and puerile posturing, the damage inflicted by those who delight in cheap barbs, insidious provocations, the proliferation of *ad hominem* attacks. We know the carnage in its wake.

BUT, there is much to be said for the collision of Catholic intellects that Cardinal John Henry Newman championed in the nineteenth century, a collision that results in deeper understanding, more sophisticated appropriations of the truth, the realization that it is often in the oppositional cauldron of debate that we mature in our grasp of the Word.

We shouldn't fear disagreement, even fiery disagreement; but what we should fear is an adversariality that is rigidly ideological and fundamentalist.

One of the most striking instances of episcopal openness occurred today when the Military Ordinary of Essen, Germany, Bishop Franz-Josef Overbeck, addressed the issue of the German Synod: its moral and theological necessity, the gravity of the relentless sex abuse crisis—a "disease never ending" with its spiraling effect on the German faithful—the consequent loss of episcopal authority, and the deluge of Catholics requesting that their baptismal certificates be invalidated. (The German state provides tax money to registered churches, like the Catholic and Lutheran, and this transfer of money is predicated on the authenticated membership of the respective denomination. By withdrawing from the lists, the financial health of the German Catholic Church is directly affected.) Overbeck spoke firmly and somewhat emotionally about the personal impacts on him as bishop: "Since I have been bishop three hundred priests have died, and I have only ordained fifteen. In addition, I faced a cataract of sex allegations against a cardinal who has been dead for thirty years. This can't continue. In Germany women in ministry involves a tense interplay of doctrine and enculturation. Our ecclesial reality in Germany demands that we find pastoral responses that help us recover our integrity."

OCTOBER 24, 2023

My seventy-fifth birthday: lunch with Cardinal Michael Czerny, SJ; no press briefing as the delegates are busily at work drafting the *Letter to the People of God*.

OCTOBER 25, 2023

If the Germans have held sway for a bit, today was America's day with the recently created cardinal and new prefect of the Dicastery of Bishops, Robert Francis Prevost, OSA, and Archbishop Timothy Broglio, military ordinary of the United States. And it was disappointing.

By contrast with Overbeck and Schönborn, the U.S. prelates were evasive and timid. They started off by apologizing for not keeping up with the work of the journalists in the room, pleading limited time because of the tight Synod agenda, but they thanked the media present for their work—a welcome first by any of the delegates to date.

Prevost acknowledged the difficulty journalists faced because of the restrictions placed on access to information but saw in the pope's intention a laudable goal that has been achieved: creating an environment wherein dialogue can flourish in an atmosphere of trust, and where listening with respect to each other can offset the toxicity we find in the public forum with its polarizing rhetoric.

The model Francis is using—deeply Ignatian in its origin and much used in Latin America in ecclesial settings, as Prevost can attest given his years as a bishop in Peru—is the perfect antidote to the poison of vitriol and intolerance that is regnant in both secular and Church circles.

Try the United States Conference of Catholic Bishops (USCCB).

Speaking of which, Christopher Lamb, Vatican affairs writer, pressed Broglio, who is the president of the USCCB, on the absence of synodality on the agenda of the last bishops' plenary. Broglio—in manner and bearing he reminds me of Cardinal Bernard Law, once of Boston and later of Rome, who presided over press briefings at the '85 Extraordinary Synod with an air of executive hauteur—responded smoothly but unpersuasively that although it wasn't on their agenda for the general meeting, it was a topic for the Executive of the USCCB Board—although they don't circulate their agenda, so, in effect, it was a hidden item.

Although the predictably contentious points surfaced—LGBTQ+, women in ministry (diaconate and presbyterate), mature married men (*viri probati*), the absence of women in ecclesial leadership—the American bishops adopted a conservationist strategy: best to conserve what we have, the tradition must be respected even if changes occur down the line, clericalizing women can create new problems, and arguing from the point of view of parallels with secular leadership fails to recognize the essential (ontological) difference that is the Church.

Prevost rightly acknowledged that three women have been added to the Dicastery of Bishops, ensuring the presence of women in one of the most important Vatican governance bodies. He also reminded the journalists that this synod is not really about any structural changes but about the charismatic or relational reality of the Church as experienced through the prism of synodality.

Although this session of guest delegates was top heavy with clerics—bishops mostly—and in that not much different from the working template employed throughout the month, the presence of one laywoman (unlike most of the other women, who are more often than not consecrated religious) was especially arresting today because she spoke from the heart, unreservedly, and with insight that rose above the mind-numbing banalities of Church-speak.

Dr. Nora Kofognotera Nonterah, a Ghanaian theologian, said that the Church should sit at the feet of laywomen in Africa in order to come to a deeper knowledge of the spiritual fecundity of living synodally:

> I came to the Synod with the hopes, the joys, the dreams, the anxieties, the lamentations, but also the

resilience of the African women....We need to give a preferential option for the laity in the educational fields of the church, like theology, canon law, the social teachings of the church, leadership ministry. This should become the norm and practice of a synodal church.

As is customary in a viscerally entrenched hierarchical Church, where the guest delegates are called upon to speak in a sequence of office, rank, and gender, Nonterah had the last word. And she outshone all the prelates present with her clarity and self-confidence. Last but not least.

The Synod has drafted and released its *Letter to the People of God*, and although inclined to the anodyne, it does reinforce the special nature of this synod and the obligations that attend on those present to enflesh the synodal experience in their home churches:

> We hope that the months leading to the Second Session in October 2024 will allow everyone to concretely participate in the dynamism of missionary communion indicated by the word "synod" [to walk together]. This is not about ideology, but about an experience rooted in the apostolic tradition...as the Pope reminded us at the beginning of this process: *communion and mission can risk remaining somewhat abstract, unless we cultivate an ecclesial praxis that expresses the concreteness of synodality....encouraging real involvement of each and all.*[3]

There was nothing anodyne, however, in an intervention by the pope the same day railing against the perfidies of clericalism. In his characteristically uncensored directness, Francis said in his native Spanish:

Clericalism is a whip, it is a scourge, it is a form of worldliness that defiles and damages the face of the Lord's bride, it enslaves God's holy and faithful people. And God's people, God's holy faithful people go forward with patience and humility, enduring the scars, mistreatment, and marginalization of institutionalized clericalism. And how naturally we speak of the princes of the church or of episcopal promotions as career advancement! The horrors of the world, the worldliness that mistreats God's holy and faithful people!

Strong language—in tone and substance quite unlike the conventional synod interventions, but bracing and necessary. It was surprising the next day to hear Timothy Radcliffe, in response to the issue of buy-in on synodality at the local level by the parochial clergy, argue for a positive alternative to the crushing demoralization felt by diocesan clergy because of the clericalism critique. He felt that drawing the diocesan clergy into a full-bodied acceptance of the synodal way of being Church can only happen when they don't feel diminished and under the cloud of suspicion. They must feel that their vocation is a treasure and not an object of scorn. Fair game.

But surely that is not the point.

Clericalism, as this pope and several of his immediate predecessors have repeated, is what Bishop Émile-Jozef De Smedt of Bruges at the First Session of the Second Vatican Council in 1962 called the "curse of clericalism." No one has denounced it more vigorously than Francis. In addition, religious order clergy have not been spared the critique and are no less prone to a reduced sense of priestly identity, although as Radcliffe knows only too well given his long history as a mendicant friar, priests who have an order identity—Jesuit, Franciscan, Salesian, Dominican, and others—are not as fragile as those who rely on their diocesan identity only.

All the Bergoglio villains are here: clerical preferment, clerical privilege, curial entitlements, ecclesiastical careerism, vaunted privilege. You see it now in the streets of Rome: cardinals retired or otherwise deferred to as princelings, seminarians in cassocks conscious of their "special" identity, honorifics aplenty, rank and dignity on regular display.

Francis is right to deplore the trappings of clericalism. Time to set the right tone in his own diocese. It is not enough to vent; it is time for action. He is, after all, the Bishop of Rome. Clerical dress in its colorful array might be good for tourists and pilgrims but Franciscan, as in Bergoglian, witness and Central Casting are not natural bedfellows. As he said in his intervention: "It is enough to go into the ecclesiastical tailor shops in Rome to see the scandal of young priests trying on cassocks and hats, or albs and lace robes."

OCTOBER 26, 2023

Today's panel was focused exclusively on ecumenism and the composition of the panel reflected that fact: Cardinal Kurt Koch, prefect of the Dicastery for Promoting Christian Unity; Iosif, Romanian Orthodox Metropolitan of Western and Southern Europe; Opoku Onyinah, of the World Pentecostal Federation; Stanislaw Gądecki, archbishop of Poznań; and Catherine Clifford, professor of systematic and historical theology, St. Paul University in Ottawa.

It is a consistent feature of the Bergoglio papacy that Assemblies of God and Pentecostal churches find a warm reception in Rome. Given the massive incursion into traditional Catholic territory—in Central and Latin America specifically, but also in the Hispanic community in the United States—of these charismatic Christian faiths, Pope Francis's efforts to better appreciate their spirituality and appeal rather than fear their growth is remarkable. And they love him for it.

The Orthodox-Catholic Dialogue remains a priority for Francis and although hampered by the jurisdictional divisions within Orthodoxy itself—Constantinople (Istanbul) pitted against Moscow, as well as the Russian war against Ukraine generating further division within Orthodoxy—Francis has to bide his time. But his personal friendship with the Ecumenical Patriarch, Bartholomew I, and the archbishop of Canterbury, Justin Welby, ensures that ecumenical matters remain close to the papal heart. In this, he has clearly built on the ecumenical breakthroughs of John Paul II and Benedict XVI.

Catherine Clifford, a member of the International Catholic-Methodist Joint Commission and a leading Canadian ecumenist, noted that Francis first mentioned synodality in light of the document *Ecclesiological and Canonical Consequences of the Sacramental Nature of the Church: Ecclesial Communion, Conciliarity and Authority*, approved by the Joint International Commission for the Theological Dialogue between the Roman Catholic Church and the Orthodox Church. This 2007 text is also known as the Ravenna Document.

Clifford highlighted the causal connection between the Synod on Synodality with the ecumenical agenda: "The desire of all the world's bishops to take on the theme of synodality as the priority for the present synodal process is the fruit of decades of reflection in a long process of maturation that has been nourished by the dialogues that go on on a regular basis between ecumenical partners."

OCTOBER 27, 2023

From ecumenism to prayer. Today's panel consisted of the two spiritual eminences who have set the tone for the synod with their holy input: Mother Maria Ignazia Angelini, of the Benedictine Monastery of Viboldone, and Father Timothy Radcliffe, of the Dominican Monastery at Oxford. Presiding serenely in the religious habits of their orders, both made clear from the outset that they were spiritual assistants to the assembly, did not have voting privileges, and did not provide formal interventions.

They did, however, provide spiritual meditations that became for many the high point of the synodal gathering. They were, with Francis, the spiritual architects of the synod.

Mother Angelina heralded the revolutionary nature of the synod with its gifts of openness, listening, and nurturing a human and not technocratic pace. Father Radcliffe also spoke about the extraordinary change in how we now do a synod. He had attended many before and they were not in the least like this one. In fact, in response to a question from the floor once again questioning whether this synod is genuinely episcopal and therefore authoritative or a hybrid construct vacant of any authority precisely because it is not exclusively episcopal, Radcliffe spoke of the new synod as more episcopal than past synods. The bishops were no longer tiered according to rank; they sat in chairs at round tables "talking and listening to their people." They were at the center and not at an isolated peak removed from the commerce of humanity.

Also present at the briefing today was Father Alois, prior of the Taizé Community, who is a "special guest" of the synod and who made a very fine point that encapsulated in a sound bite the goal of a synodal Church where all the faithful "listen and *live* joy in simplicity."

OCTOBER 28, 2023

The last days of the synod were occupied with the crafting of the *Synthesis Report: A Synodal Church in Mission*, and predictably the politics of composition were paramount—at least at the beginning. Protracted discussions, surfacing differences, scrupulously if not always competently exercised control by the press office mandarins, and media folk desperate for something concrete to write about, combined to make for a hothouse environment—but only for those with entrée to it.

Eventually the document surfaced, following a detailed vote by the synod members paragraph by paragraph so that a strong statement could be issued that enjoyed strong majority support—and in that they were successful. But at a cost.

The *Synthesis* is mostly generic in tone, avoids any kind of polarizing polemic, attempts to bridge rather than demarcate, and outlines what must come down the line. Divided up—as per other daily summaries—into "Convergences," "Matters for Consideration," and "Proposals" ("Divergences" now deemed inappropriate language), the final document of the First Session makes some telling points that speak to the hopes of the assembly, the lessons learned, the encounters treasured, and the bruises borne. Here are ten takeaways:

- It is clear that some people are afraid that they will be forced to change; others fear that nothing at all will change or that there will be too little courage to move at the pace of the living Tradition. Also, perplexity and opposition can sometimes conceal a fear of losing power and the privileges that derive from it.
- Each local church is encouraged to equip itself with suitable people trained to facilitate and accompany processes of ecclesial discernment.
- The experiences of encounter, sharing a common life, and serving those living in poverty and on the margins should be an integral part of all formation paths by Christian communities: It is a requirement of faith, not an optional extra. *This is especially true*

for candidates for ordained ministry and consecrated life (italics are mine).

- New paradigms are needed for pastoral engagement with Indigenous peoples, taking the form of a common journey and not an action done to them or for them.
- The expression "an all-ministerial Church," used in the *Instrumentum laboris*, can lend itself to misunderstanding. Its meaning will have to be clarified in order to remove any ambiguities.
- Different opinions have been expressed about priestly celibacy. Its value is appreciated by all as richly prophetic and a profound witness to Christ: some ask, however, whether its appropriateness, theologically, for priestly ministry should necessarily translate into a disciplinary obligation in the Latin Church, above all in ecclesial and cultural contexts that make it more difficult. *This discussion is not new but requires further discussion* (italics are mine).
- It is necessary to implement, in forms legally yet to be defined, structures and processes for regular review of each bishop's performance, with reference to the style of his authority, the economic administration of the diocese's assets, and the functioning of participatory bodies, as well as safeguarding against all possible kinds of abuse. A culture of accountability is an integral part of a synodal Church that promotes coresponsibility.
- In light of the teachings of Vatican II, it is necessary to carefully evaluate whether it is opportune to ordain the prelates of the Roman curia as bishops.
- Sometimes the anthropological categories we have developed are not able to grasp the complexity of

the elements emerging from experience or knowledge in the sciences and require greater precision and further study.

- Considering the synodal practices of the first millennium, we suggest a study exploring how ancient institutions can be recovered in the current canonical order, and harmonizing them with newly created ones, such as episcopal conferences.

Timothy Radcliffe sagely observed of the synod process itself in one of his meditations that the bravest thing we can do in this synod is to be truthful about our convictions but also about our doubts and questions, the questions to which we have no clear answers. Then we shall draw near as fellow searchers, disciples, beggars for the truth. In Graham Greene's *Monsignor Quixote*, a Spanish Catholic priest and a communist mayor make a holiday together. One day they dare to share their doubts. The priest says, "It is odd how sharing a sense of doubt can bring men together perhaps even more than sharing a faith. The believer will fight another believer over a shade of difference; the doubter fights only with himself."

Timothy Radcliffe's many references to the British novelist's priest figures—"the whisky priest" of *The Power and the Glory*, for example—as well as the eponymous Monsignor Quixote (he omits mention of the "guerilla priest," Leon Rivas of *The Honorary Consul*)—underscores the important role the priest plays in Greene's fiction. The *alter Christus*, or other Christ, serves as a metaphor for the broken one, the failure redeemed by grace, heroic self-sacrifice, and expansive love. For instance, Monsignor Quixote throughout his priestly ministry drew again and again for spiritual nourishment from those writers and mystics—Thérèse Martin, John of the Cross, and Francis de Sales—who wrote of love rather than of law and abstruse theological concepts. He despised the tradition of the manualists. Not for him a Catholic morality bound to the tyranny of canonists. In a conversation with his own long-suffering and exasperated bishop, Quixote shows how the polite world of ecclesiastical diplomacy and gentility founders before the blunt command of charity:

> "The Church always struggles to keep above politics."
> "Always?"
> "You know very well what I thought of your unfortunate involvement with the organization In Vinculis."
> "It was an impromptu act of charity, Excellency. I admit that I didn't really think. Perhaps with charity one shouldn't think. Charity, like love, should be blind."

It is the blindness of such love, its ingenuousness, that accounts for the monsignor's ready sympathy with the doomed, like the thief whom he helps to escape the *Guardia Civil* and who thanklessly steals his shoes. In the end such love as this, *diakonia*, prepares him ultimately for *kenosis* (self-emptying love), the love of a *compañero* offering an invisible host with the Salesian utterance: "by this hopping." It is not a wild comparison to note that Greene's fictional Monsignor Quixote is Bergoglian in some striking instances: Monsignor Quixote is considered suspect because he prefers God's love to God's justice and pastoral compassion to the norms of moral theology, and his bishop sees him as a source of great scandal, a dangerous simpleton. Francis has his detractors too, fearful of his unalterable privileging of experience over ideas, mercy over judgment.

Wrestling with doubt is the honest believer's quotidian struggle. Taking doubt into the aula is not a banner of weakness but a testimony to the limitations of certitude. Francis values reason and strongly held convictions, but recognizes the supremacy of humility in the human quest to embrace the Ineffable, to track the Divine in our lives and loves.

OCTOBER 28, 2023, EVENING

Tonight I gave a talk—"The Revolutionary Synod and Why We Need It"—to the community I have been living with this past month: the Missionary Oblates of Mary Immaculate. The room was full—graduate students from the pontifical universities, canonists and theologians, guests, rectors and subordinate staff, and a healthy smattering of undergraduate theology students—and it was an invigorating evening with stiff but respectful questions, curiosity-bred commentaries on the synod buzz, and playful banter around the synod's personnel makeup (one of the bishop delegates, an Oblate who is always masterfully cloaked in Namibian vesture and possessed of an infectious laugh accompanied by his naturally jolly disposition, provided ample confirmation of my own observations).

This community has fed me, provided transportation, cared for my welfare, and sustained me in times of unbearable heat, media frustrations, and the incurable inefficiencies of Roman civil governance.

They are a treasure.

OCTOBER 29, 2023

The concluding Mass with Francis presiding was actually in St. Peter's Basilica this time rather than in the piazza with its elaborate opening, relentless sun beaming down on the masses—including the unsheltered media atop the porticos, and the seemingly endless procession.

There is a special alcove in the Basilica for the media, so Tom Reese, Jesuit political scientist and commentator on the Holy See, and I were directed by several officials—not all working from the same playbook—to our special spot. The routing was

Byzantine. Once we arrived at our designated spot, I observed, to my horror, that there was room for forty comfortably, or at least manageably, but three times that number were crammed in. Very few seats, the most comfortable and prominent occupied by the CEO of Salt + Light Media, with the rest of the space occupied by a gaggle of young videographers, a platoon of audio journalists, and a remnant of print scribblers. I had to sit on the floor—a spot I jealously guarded against intruders—and when I did have to stand, for those appropriate ritual moments, I was inadvertently whacked on the head with a mobile film apparatus of substantial weight. I think I may have been mercifully concussed because I don't remember the rest of the liturgy, including the homily.

OCTOBER 31, 2023

Flight back to Toronto today. *Arrivederci Roma.*
Corny, I know.

III

THE INTERREGNUM

To ENSURE THAT the momentum of the synod does not dissipate between the two sessions—*entre les séances*—and that these months are used productively, Francis ordered the creation of study groups tasked with exploring in depth various themes that surface in the *Synthesis Report* and that call for serious reflection. These groups constitute "laboratories of synodality" and they are charged to "walk together, listening to the Holy Spirit, not only during the conduct of the Assembly, but also in the implementation of its orientations."[1]

For sure, various ecclesiastical jurisdictions have been continuing the synodal undertaking with a commendable, if tense, seriousness. The Irish Church's Synodal Pathway is but one of them, and a model for others. And yet, all evidence points to a general hierarchical entropy, a reluctance to get truly serious about synodality, and an entrenched commitment to the status quo, regardless of the rhetoric—an entropy that certainly defined the U.S. and Canadian responses, preoccupied as they were with their national Eucharistic Congress and plans for the 2025 Jubilee Year, respectively.

The Second Session must address the torpor at the top if it is to mobilize the masses at the bottom. Or perhaps that is the Francis vision steeped in Newman: release the energies of the laity to save the Church.

IV

THE SECOND SESSION

October 2024

OCTOBER 1, 2024

Although tonight's penitential Vigil in the basilica was a moving and strategic event—addressing through diverse speakers many of the abuses suffered by members of the Church and often inflicted by the Church itself through its ministers and teachings—it was in part overshadowed by what for many is the key challenge facing the Church. That is, how it recognizes, incorporates, and innovates—cognizant of its fidelity to the living tradition of the Church—the role of women in/and ministry.

Questions around Francis's often archaic views of women get in the way of seriously broaching the deeper matter of inclusion, a vital and relevant anthropology, and the formidable challenges confronting a Church that appears to relegate women to a secondary status in matters ecclesiastical.

OCTOBER 2, 2024

The usual: frantic drivers, occasional bouts of organization, and endless streams of tourists and pilgrims; the welcome: temperate weather in sharp contrast with last year's debilitating heat and old friends reconnecting; the synod mood: a potpourri of caution, anxiety, hope, and wild expectation.

On the same day that the synod formally opened with a solemn pontifical Mass with several thousands in attendance, a small group of women—including representatives from the Canadian Network for Women's Equality (CNWE)—staged a gentle, humor-laced, and earnest demonstration on the Lungotevere Costello near the Castel Sant'Angelo, variously a papal citadel, residence, and prison. The group was stating their opposition to the exclusion of women from ordained ministry—diaconal and presbyteral.

While watching the protestors kick their empty tin cans (which they dubbed their "vati-cans"), I noticed two young cassock-wearing clerics walk by them with studied indifference, if not a smirk of condescension.

And that is clerical Rome.

Many Catholics, including a significant number of the synod delegates or voting members, were dismayed when the decision was made to redirect the issue of holy orders and women to one of the pope's ten study groups for further examination. In addition, the Dicastery for the Doctrine of the Faith has been charged to prepare a document for Francis on the basis of the study group's exploratory work but has already indicated "that there is no room for a positive decision by the Magisterium regarding the access of women to the diaconate, understood as a degree of the Sacrament of Holy Orders." And yet strangely, perhaps as a conciliatory gesture or as a benign stalling tactic, the study group report observes that "the Dicastery judges that the opportunity to continue the work of an in-depth study remains open."

In part, this thinking is driven by the perception that women *qua* women exercise power differently than men, and to that end the dicastery will study the lives of great women of the Church to ascertain their spiritual *modus operandi* without the benefit of holy orders.

The list includes Matilda of Canossa, Hildegard of Bingen, Bridget of Sweden, Catherine of Siena, Joan of Arc, Teresa of Avila, Juana Inés de la Cruz, Mama Antula, Elizabeth Ann Seton, Dorothy Day, Madeline Delbrêl, Armida Barelli, and Maria Montessori.

All eminent; all securely dead.

Missing from the list—and, of course, no list could possibly be exhaustive—are Julian of Norwich, who often addressed God in feminine terms, and Thérèse de Lisieux, who actually yearned to be a priest.

The question about women and ministry cannot be decided by the synod, whose function is essentially advisory to the pontiff, but it can serve as a forum, a platform, an environment of respectful dialogue, intense listening, and mature discernment. Those qualities, much in evidence last year, need to bear fruit—to produce results that are not enshrouded in secrecy nor motivated by fear.

That takes courage and it takes trust.

Timothy Radcliffe spoke frankly about the challenges we face as a Church, and asked at the end of one of his meditations: "What new ministries are needed for the church to recognize their authority and commission them to exercise it? The Gospel sheds light on so many who acted with authority in that time [including Mary Magdalene, the apostle to the apostles]. May we do so today."

Radcliffe is not staking out a position; he is securing a portal. That is his irenic way.

But I wonder if ordination is not premature when we still have to address, as Bishop De Smedt of Bruges once called it, the "curse of clericalism."

OCTOBER 3, 2024

Today's inaugural press briefing, held in its traditional location on the Via della Conciliazione—it had been relocated last year because of renovations—was a welcome moment on some fronts and a disappointing reprise of last year's early media encounters on other fronts.

The welcome news consisted of upgraded facilities, easier access to translation devices, comfortable chairs, and a pleasing backdrop. The disappointing bits consisted of the usual choreography of slippery rhetoric; muddled oversight by senior operatives of the Dicastery of Communications; protracted evasions around questions that involve embargo, secrecy, and transparency; as well as the nondisclosure of names (principal speakers and authors) that actually help make the work of journalists possible.

The delegate members that composed this first of many press conferences included: two special secretaries of the Synod Secretariat; the president delegate for the session, Sister Maria de Los Dolores Palencia Gómez; the prefect of communications; and most importantly the diminutive ecclesiastical U.S. powerhouse of quiet eloquence, temperate response, and clear sightedness, Daniel Flores of Brownsville, Texas.

In his short reflection—in sharp contrast with the verbose secretaries—Flores noted that "perspective is not the enemy of the truth. That is why we have FOUR gospels. Trees grow in the dark and we don't see that growth as it happens. We wait until the morning and see it in the light." Best definition of the synodal process I can find yet: succinct, poetic, and fresh.

OCTOBER 4, 2024

In stunning contrast with yesterday's emollient approach by Flores to the contentious issues that will surface in a trusting and respectful environment like the Synod on Synodality, today we had the forthright approach of Bishop Antony Randazzo, representing the Federation of Catholic Bishops' Conferences of Oceania, and not one inclined to grant quarter.

He excoriated the West for its failure to arrest the destruction inflicted on the many discrete jurisdictions that make up the vast territory that is Oceania—rising sea levels, massive inundations of fertile land, vicious storms that wreak wide damage, uncontrolled migration disruptions, etcetera—by reminding the Church in Europe and North America that this is a new colonialism with the Church emulating a business model approach and choosing the discourse of finance, like *networking*, over theological language, like *communio*.

Randazzo was fired up with a prophetic righteousness that was a marvel to behold in an otherwise tepid and uninteresting press briefing.

But when he was later queried by a reporter from CNS on the matter of sacramental ministry and women, he launched into a parallel attack condemning this "Western obsession with a niche issue. We are not dealing with the vast majority of women whose status is second class." Randazzo deplores the influence of a small group of progressives from the West to, in effect, sabotage the synod's larger remit.

Someone should tell the fiery prelate that it is not a zero-sum game. The Church can deal with both the challenges posed by the disenfranchised and by those eager for a greater inclusion of women in ministry.

OCTOBER 5, 2024

One of the peculiar, constant, and irritating features of the daily press briefings is the insistence by the overseers that things be explained to the reporters, journalists, and academics as if they were incapable of grasping the content. They digest the synod discussions of the day, identify the themes, and summarize the essential points—points that they determine. It is all rather condescending and controlling.

But they don't manage what happens *at* the press conference. They can be as illumined, surprised, and emotionally moved as the crowd of scribblers they serve. For instance, the Maronite bishop Mounir Khairallah's heartrending plea for peace in war-ravaged Lebanon set a new tone for anguished outrage. Similarly, Launay Saturné, a Haitian archbishop, outlined in depth the daily struggle of his people for a scrap of food, a scrap of security, a scrap of human dignity.

Catherine Clifford, the eminent ecumenical theologian, asked the pointed question: Why have the vast majority of Catholic dioceses not experienced a local synod in the sixty years since the end of the council? Especially germane when you consider that by 2050, 70–75 percent of the world's Christians will be resident in the Southern Hemisphere. A new global Church is in the making in our time.

Perhaps the most important thing that happened today for me was not the press briefing but what awaited me outside the Stampa. While waiting for a bus on a day when the city was once again disrupted by a public transportation strike that was wildcat, unpredictable, perplexing, and spotty, I could not help but notice that amidst the large crowds waiting for the occasional bus there was a man lying prostrate on the ground adjacent to the Vatican wall. I wasn't particularly concerned about him as he had been upright earlier, delighted in smoking his cigarettes, and then would recline again. When some of the passing citizens and endlessly patient bus clients stopped and spoke with him, he would turn on them, shout loudly that he didn't want to be disturbed, and then go back to his rotating pattern of sitting erect punctuated by lying flat.

What struck me most, though, was the makeup of those who

were solicitous about his state of being, although at a distance. Several clerics walked by him without even giving him a glance—and their number consisted mostly of Franciscan friars—while the one person who actually knelt in front of him, held his hand, and whispered in his ear—in other words, made personal contact with him—was a young woman in a hijab.

The Good Samaritan parable enacted at a bus stop.

OCTOBER 7, 2024

At today's briefing, mention was made of the Good Samaritan as a symbol of mercy and the synodal path. Too bad yesterday's passersby at the bus stop—*Franciscani* in particular—missed this lesson.

Sister Mary Theresa Barron, president of the International Union of Superiors General, a large, global, and formidable group—who distinguished herself at last year's session as I noted at the time—spoke persuasively of the "deeper quality of listening" currently in the aula. She also raised the point: "What do we do when we have passionate convictions that are not aligned with the Will of God?" This is Church speak for finding a way to accommodate your beliefs to a greater end. Suck it up, in other words.

Repeatedly, reporters and analysts raise the seemingly insuppressible issue of holy orders and women in spite of efforts by the communications people and the presenters to keep it off the official agenda. For the moment, that is. Until next time. An opportune time. Down the road.

Like his colleague Antony Randazzo, Archbishop Gintaras Grušas—president of the Consilium Conferentiarum Episcoporum Europae—betrayed a mite of impatience when he said that "we must not let one issue dominate resulting in the exclusion of other ministries and vocational calls."

Perhaps the time is right to realize, as Canadian religious educator Michael Dallaire notes in his book *Soundings on Eucharist and Priesthood* (2024), that "a call to the priesthood is not based on one's culture, race, gender, sexual orientation, or marital status....It is the *core* of the person that is called, as priesthood is rooted in the *heart* of a person who experiences Christ as 'the source and summit' of life and who has experienced a call, a summons, to lead a Christian community in the living of the Christian story."

OCTOBER 8, 2024

Jim Martin, SJ, and Michael J. O'Loughlin, both of *Outreach: An LGBTQ Catholic Resource*, scheduled a panel conversation today in the aula of the Jesuit Generalate. The session—open to invited guests and closed to the media, although the presence of the latter was quite noticeable—was designed to provide a safe and supportive place to discuss the experience of being a gay Catholic.

Voices from Chile, Zimbabwe, England and Wales, Uganda, and Malta combined to provide a rich symphony of perspectives. The panelists spoke with candor, passion, pain, and joy and, without exception—whether sexually abused by a cleric, persecuted in their own countries, or subject to social and religious incomprehension and hostility—they expressed a deep and visceral connection with their Catholic faith, cradle and convert alike.

This initiative, an *America Media* ministry, is premised on the conviction that listening to the other is fundamental to acceptance, that when people interact with Catholics of alternate sexualities their eyes will be opened and they will avoid easy judgment.

In other words, it is bridge-building; it is not an academic exercise, collective psychotherapy, or ideological lobbying. It is grounded in respectful listening—very synodal in conception and execution.

The deeper questions, though—around revisiting a biblical anthropology, erasing an archaic ontology, and reconceptualizing a Catholic sexual ethics that is not biologistic—have still to be addressed by the universal Church.

I had lunch with a cardinal who is very close to the pope, and he was querying me on where I thought Francis originated his idea of synodality—context, history, etymology. It was more test than interrogation and did reveal one important thing for both of us: It is a concept that has meaning in its making. It is not a finished product. It is a process wherein trust is paramount.

OCTOBER 9, 2024

The Reverend Deacon Geert de Cubber has no time for preparing for a soft landing. He lands his remarks on point and if that landing shakes up his hearers then that is as it should be.

Decidedly *not* in clericals, the permanent deacon from Dutch-speaking Belgium observed that "if the church in his country does not become a synodal church it will not survive as a Belgian church." Once again, the Church has been ravaged by the clerical sex abuse crisis, far from resolved, dispiriting, and catastrophic. The Belgian Church is "old, tired and uncertain of the future," but De Cubber is no hostage to despair.

Firmly rooted in his family life—his wife and three children supported his attendance as a delegate at the synod, and if they had expressed no interest in doing so he would have declined his election as a synod delegate—De Cubber oversees both the youth and communications departments of his diocese (Ghent), and he is unswerving in his dedication to his dual vocation as a parent and as a minister of service. Priesthood, he insists, is not his vocation and he fears the clericalization of the Church. But most importantly he fears the trivialization of the Church's witness. As he says, "The Katholic Church is on a Kamino."

OCTOBER 10, 2024

Chris White, of the *National Catholic Reporter*, is a well-connected Vaticanista. He knows the old guard and he knows the new guard, he is comfortable in his knowledge of Italian and the *mores* of the Romans—both profane and sacred, and he knows how to laugh at the petty absurdities that get in the way of a rational life.

Over coffee this morning we reveled in the gossip, got caught up on the latest doings of colleagues, took pleasure in the memory of our mutual friend and veteran Vaticanista the redoubtable Rob Mickens, and lamented the sorry state of American politics.

And then it was over.

But the festive mood was only interrupted, not finished. Later in the evening at the Ristorante Scarpone on the Via S. Pancrazio in the tony area of Rome under the generous auspices of an Australian delegation of laity—led by the marvelously connected Mark O'Connor, a Marist Brother, the communications brain behind the Diocese of Parramatta, and a Francis Fellow at Newman College, University of Melbourne. There were prelates, cardinals, both retired and active, and most importantly a bevy of engaged, curious, probing, and irreverent journalists.

The Vatican is all about whispers and intrigue—that is the Hollywood version, and it isn't without validity. But that is only part of the story. There is also the healthy air of keen questioning, fundamental loyalty to the tradition, confidential sharing, and deep collegial cooperation that also describe the Vatican machinery and those who cover that beat.

That was much in evidence tonight.

OCTOBER 11, 2024

Much more than hollow jabber and the daily drone today. At the press conference, Joe Tobin, cardinal archbishop of Newark, New Jersey, is one of the most naturally amiable prelates I have ever met: warm, inviting, comfortable with the laity—women and men, unafraid to respond to the tough questions, although he has his periphrastic moments. A steady and encouraging Francis ally for turning us into a synodal Church.

In addressing not only the spirit but the mechanics of synodality, Tobin alluded to the stellar work of peace activist Alec Reid. A Redemptorist priest, like Tobin, Reid was critical to the success of the Good Friday Peace Agreement of 1998 that brought an end to the Troubles that began in Northern Ireland in 1968. Tobin recounted how he once asked Reid how he did it: Bring centuries-encrusted hate to the table of conciliation.

Reid insisted on two nonnegotiable items: (1) everyone had to be at the table; (2) women must be at the table.

The accords were actually signed in a Redemptorist monastery.

What Reid did in Northern Ireland, Francis is doing with synodality: bringing people who hold discordant views to a common table and demonstratively showcasing women in the process.

Shane Mackinlay, bishop of Sandhurst, Australia, is rapidly gaining attention as a cleric who listens to the people he serves, fully endorses the role of synods as a means of Church-shaping, and retains the wonderful air of Aussie informality that sets him apart from the stuffy Romanized hierarchs—those with the George Pell personnel residue that hold prominent Sees on the east coast, particularly the Dominican powerhouse, Anthony Fisher of Sydney.

Mackinlay has degrees in physics and theology and that nice combination will have natural appeal for Francis, an erstwhile chemistry aspirant.

At *pranzo* today, I entertained—and was in turn entertained by—someone else with a taste for science and theology: Julian Paparella. Having studied biology and theology at McGill University, in addition to studying at the Institut Catholique de Paris, he is resident of Rome with his family and child, pursuing advanced work at the reconstructed and revisioned Pontifical John Paul II Theological Institute for Marriage and Family Sciences at the Lateran University.

Paparella's special interest, the subject of his doctoral research, is on what the Church and theology can learn by listening to Indigenous families in Canada.

In an article published in the *Journal of Moral Theology*, Paparella quotes an Australian Aboriginal, Lilla Watson, who writes regarding non-Indigenous who have come in any number of ways to support the Indigenous and their many causes that "if you come to help me, you are wasting your time. If you have come because your liberation is bound up with mine, then let us work together."

Is there a better description of the synodal process than this?

OCTOBER 12, 2024

On this very day I encountered two strikingly different perspectives on the Church, the synod, and the pope that were predictable to some degree, refreshingly insightful in many instances, but on one matter these discordant voices aligned, and I found that disturbing. Both men are accomplished in their respective fields, each with an impressive academic pedigree, decades of familiarity with the Roman scene, shapers in the communications and academic environments, and steadfast believers in a time of unsettling flux.

The publisher: a staunch advocate for ultraconservative

Catholics, specifically devoted to the Franciscan charismatics of the Middle Ages, to the life and legacy of undiluted G. K. Chesterton, and to a gaggle of Catholic figures of dubious credibility—including the renegade Jesuit Joe Fessio and the excommunicated former prelate and nuncio, Carlo Maria Viganò. The publisher is rooted in the Catholic tradition's rich history, if selectively, and engaging to speak with. He is a layperson.

The academic: a fervent critic of the Church's institutional failures, most importantly on the clerical sex abuse issue, the Church's self-inflicted impoverishment by excluding women from ordained ministries, and of the daily corruptions that infect official Church life in Rome. He is a bridge-builder with other faith traditions, an eloquent embodiment of the Catholic genius for synthesis and meaningful dialogue. The academic is a wonderful host with refined gustatorial tastes. He is a priest.

Where the two converge is on the matter of the Bergoglio papacy. From both perspectives, he is a disappointment. Grumpy, capricious, unforthcoming, autocratic, and ungenerous. Wow.

They have their own reasons for their shared assessment. I happen not to agree with them, but because neither is an intellectual dilettante nor a professional firebrand, and because they amass their arguments on the basis of both empirical and anecdotal data, it is not easy, nor desirable, to discount them.

One faults Francis for his notion of synodality and the other for his failure to live up to it.

OCTOBER 14, 2024

The summary we get of the interventions and discussion points held at the morning session prior to our afternoon briefing is delivered in a spluttering style that is difficult for the translators, and more difficult still for the journalists. The droning has a strangely soporific effect so that the scattered content goes largely unnoticed.

Clever ruse.

But we could glean two things from the ninety interventions (a strikingly large number) that remind us that no matter what other issues surface during the synod, the role of women and the devastating crisis around clerical sex abuse are constants.

In this instance the two elided, as the scandal of priests abusing women religious—the acute vulnerability of cloistered nuns in particular—was spoken about, and this with the Rupnik affair hovering in the background as unfinished papal business.

Édouard Sinayobe, bishop of Cyangugu, Rwanda, reminded the gathered writers of the jarring reality of the genocide that nearly destroyed his country and that the consequences of this destructive event continue to be felt. Rwanda's own synodal experience is key to reconciliation, restorative justice, and holistic healing.

That is the particular. And now to the general.

But the question that was aired but not answered in relation to synods, period, was the question that won't—can't—go away: "Would a local synod that allowed women in the diaconate be a legitimate exercise in plurality or a shattering of communion?"

OCTOBER 15, 2024

Robert Choiniere, a New York–based but now relocated to California Ignatian facilitator and lay leader, who cannot abide a day without eggs and therefore for whom an American breakfast is imperative, returns to Rome with a cohort of university students determined to give them a taste of synodality. They love it.

Choiniere is a strong believer in synodality—as a concept, a working principle, a way of being. To that end, he has participated in synodality exercises, parish conscientization retreats, and seminars designed to motivate youth to embrace this new way of *ecclesia*. His vade mecum, *The Engaged Parish: A Practical Guide to Creating a Community of Spiritual Discernment*, embodies the spirituality of synodality skillfully admixed with Ignatian spirituality. A special Francis cocktail.

Like with the majority of Americans present—theological experts, media personnel, synod delegates, and curious pilgrims—the imminent U.S. presidential election hangs over their heads, daily amassing a hurricane of increasing dread.

Choiniere is especially concerned that so much that has been gained in recent decades in the areas of respect for sexual orientation, same-sex civil marriages, transgender rights, and others are all up for sale if the MAGA crowd secures the highest power in the land. Some five hundred pieces of legislation—state and federal—curtailing sexual rights can be quickly enacted.

But this synod is more about hope and trust than dread and fear, although other political headwinds batter the aula: the worsening situation in the Middle East with its relentless carnage, the deadly stalemate between Ukraine and its Russian invader, the global migration turmoil, and the dire aftershocks of climate upheaval. And that is as it should be and as Francis wants it: The world is not something we flee from; it is our home, and its cries for mercy, for a benevolent hearing, must be heard.

Today's press briefing underscores the above: the cruel, methodical destruction of the Amazon, the depletion of water resources, and the rape of the ecosystem were all in the commentary provided by the Franciscan cardinal archbishop of Manaus, Brazil, Leonardo Ulrich Steiner. He spoke of the pressing need for a hermeneutic of wholeness based on a nurturing rather than despoiling approach to the environment, our common home.

When pressed on the issue of the ordination of the *viri probati*, mature married men, that was a hot topic at the Synod on Amazonia, Steiner laconically observed: "We have not gone sufficiently forward."

In response to a reporter's question about women and the diaconate—you know, the topic no one is to address—Steiner spoke of the work being done in the interior of his vast diocese by women: proclaiming the gospel, preaching, providing a sacramental presence.

Steiner concluded his remarks—the vast majority of questions were addressed to him—by musing, "Why not restore the female diaconate? This role could complement that of the male deacons. The issue is not a matter of gender but vocation."

I have given numerous retreats on the wounded spirituality of Henri Nouwen to permanent deacons and their wives—in Albany, Rochester, Spokane, Kingston, London, Sault Ste Marie—and in every instance, and I mean every, the deacons would admit that their wives were the ones who most authentically lived their ministry of service and that they should be the ones ordained.

If their bishops shared this sentiment, there was little public evidence of it, just a polite and political silence.

OCTOBER 16, 2024

Last year Catholic traditionalists and conservatives—and they are not quite the same thing, although they share many common convictions around institutional drift and papal dysfunction, as they see it—tenaciously questioned the daily presenters from the synod on the authority of that very body to think of changing what Divine Revelation had deposited for the Church.

Again and again they asked their wearied interlocutors why the Church would encourage talk and expectations around doctrinal change that Revelation and Tradition forbid.

Well, that group is back but the coloration of the crowd is different: young men, canon lawyers, American zealots—and all not inclined to take prisoners.

The Pillar is an online news magazine with its two principal editors/writers, J. D. Flynn and Ed Conlon, credentialed canon lawyers with a Savonarola-like passion for pure truth. They have no qualms outing clerics who live double lives and pursue all forms of ecclesiastical venality regardless of the prominence of the investigated subject.

Today, J. D. Flynn asked the Australian theologian Ormond Rush, "How does one do moral theology in a synodal way that is still in continuity with Revelation?" Flynn intended to nail if not embarrass Rush, and the latter, a conciliatory soul, quickly dispatched his opinion on the Living Tradition and then effected a civil withdrawal from the lists.

Not appeased by Rush's response, Flynn, whose approach is neither rough nor pugilistic (he is no MAGA thug after all) chose to follow up his truncated encounter with online commentary in which speaking about dangerously empowered episcopal conferences and continental "ecclesial assemblies" he writes: "Any reader of *The Pillar* can see what that would actually lead to. It's a call to see doctrine subverted by definitive interpretation, by which 'hard teachings' need not be accepted in 'cultural contexts' critical of them."

And you don't need to be a reader of *The Pillar* to figure out what is afoot in this dissenting camp of reactionaries.

The Pillarites are here for the long term.

OCTOBER 17, 2024

Nothing like a bracing shock in the morning. While reading my online edition of the *Globe and Mail* I happened upon an article by education reporter Caroline Alfonso chronicling a story of such astonishing insensitivity I found myself holding my cappuccino with a less-than-steady hand.

It would appear that school trustees at the Brant Haldimand Norfolk Catholic District School Board spent $140,000 last July traveling to Italy (four of them in total, including their Chair) to purchase statues and sculptures for their new high school, St. Padre Pio.

Do they know nothing about:

- The controversies around Pio of Pietrelcina;
- The damning Agostino Gemelli Report;
- The shelving of the *cause* by Paul VI;
- The reopening and fast-tracking of the *cause* by John Paul II?

Do they not know of any Canadian saints—including the canonization of Marie-Léonie Paradis this coming weekend in Rome?

Are they unaware of Canadian artists and sculptors of established reputation?

At a time when Catholic education is frequently under the gun, the behavior of these trustees is scandalous and scandalously stupid.

Bit of a shock at the press conference as well. One of the presenters, Gérald Cyprien Cardinal Lacroix, primate of the Canadian Church, archbishop of Quebec City, and a prelate who enjoys the confidence of the pope and the respect of his peers, spoke aimlessly in a circular fashion about synodality—at no time situating it within the context of his Quebecois and Canadian experience. And this in stark contrast with other prelate-presenters, who spoke freely of the historical challenges in their respective Sees.

Why pass up the opportunity to investigate the subtle convergences between synodality and the way Indigenous peoples dialogue, spiritually discern, and inch their way toward reconciliation?

A colleague who knows him suggests that he was chastened by the charge of sexual molestation leveled at him in 2023. He was cleared by a Vatican probe under a retired civil justice and returned to his leadership of Quebec City in 2024. But the process of accusation and legal discharge rattled him. As indeed it would any.

But he missed a teaching moment today, choosing abstract meanderings over embodied realities.

OCTOBER 18, 2024

Cardinal Stephen Ameyu Martin Mulla, archbishop of Juba in South Sudan, did today what Lacroix failed to do yesterday. He spoke about synodality in the context of his new country's pitiless war of the two generals, the massive disruptions generated by human displacement, the submerging of whole towns and villages by rising waters in one part of the country and the savage desertification wrought by droughts in other parts of the country, and all of this contributing to economic and social crises of relentless ferocity.

And yet, in the midst of this, he affirmed the role of synodality at the parish level and the fact that this is a process unending, crafting a horizon of hope.

OCTOBER 19–22, 2024

Let's call it the *Bastille Moment*. The synod delegates were invited to meet with the ten study groups established by Francis and the Synod Secretariat—a one-on-one encounter designed to lift any veil of secrecy and ensure that the operations within the synod conformed to the model of synodality being espoused for the larger *ecclesia*.

But can a leopard easily change its spots?

When the delegates arrived for their various tête-à-têtes, all seemed well, save for the meeting with group 5. Essentially, there wasn't one. The cardinal of the Dicastery for the Doctrine of the Faith who had been specifically charged with the group's mandate—to explore issues and debates around ministry and women, most specifically the ordained diaconate—discharged his responsibility to be present to two underlings. They were to take notes and politely encourage interested parties (read: everyone) to email the dicastery with their opinions.

This did not go down well.

Outraged delegates wanted explanations: Why the absence of Cardinal Fernandez? Why the refusal to release the names of the group? Why the mindless fudging, evasions, and subterfuge? Why is this non-synodal way of operating tolerated?

One delegate told me that the very credibility of the Vatican's commitment to synodality is on the line. Inarguable, I would think.

Throughout the synod's long gestation—three years in total—I have been moved by the integrity of the delegates, the pope's own radical pledge to make the Church a synodal reality, the careful academic analyses of past historical records and current interpretations in light of new knowledge, and the genuine openness to the workings of the Holy Spirit, however that is articulated.

And as a past commentator on various Church personalities, synods, and ecclesial gatherings I am not unaware of the numerous pathologies that get in the way of the ideal—the fractures of structure, the wounds of people, the fears that accomplish any diminution of power—corporate or individual, the subtle and sometimes flagrant hypocrisies that mar our best intentions.

So we need to call it out when we fail to abide by what we proclaim, when our behavior is at marked divergence from our professed convictions.

I have made my own clumsy, tentative, achingly modest

efforts to listen deeply, to reverence the other, to rest in silence before speaking and to be open to change. It doesn't come naturally. I am a polished magisterial type with a gift for prolixity and love for the grand rhetorical flourish and that is, I suppose, good in itself but it is insufficient. The synodal way is instructing me in how to rise above these insufficiencies.

Permit me to be precise. As you may recall, I have been opposed to the ordination of women on the grounds that our primary task is to radically, and I mean radically, reconceive how the diaconate and the presbyterate can be shorn of the clericalism that infects them. I think our biggest and most immediate challenge as a universal Church is to address the enduring sex abuse crisis. Again and again throughout the two synod sessions bishops and others have spoken of the devastating consequences to the Church's witness—its credibility, its efficaciousness—by the scandals that sunder it. Whether at the press briefings or in private, the bishops' anguish and confusion are painful. They seem incapable of imagining a way forward, and the pope and his advisors merely tinker with inadequate reforms.

Why ordain women into such a system at this point in our history, I have argued? Do we actually believe that they will root out clericalism rather than be corrupted by it?

Strong language, I know, but necessary to hear at this critical juncture in our history. But I have been rethinking my blanket opposition by listening, respectfully attending, the other in conversation. A Flemish permanent deacon, Geert De Cubber of Ghent, and a young married woman and mother from a group called Discerning Deacons, whose name I neglected to get but whose personal charisma I will not forget, spoke to me in eloquent terms about why women deacons are important. Their position was firmly cognizant of the relevant history, respectful of the tradition, cognizant of the pastoral reality on the ground—in this they went no further than Cardinal Steiner of Manaus—and at the same time aware of the seductive power of the clerical mentality.

They persuaded me with the logic of the heart. More Pascal than Descartes. And we need both. But the formation structure must not replicate the seminary model. If an alternative to the clerical incubation program can be developed, then the time is indeed ripe. But this is a nonnegotiable item in my view. Incorporation into the current male structure cannot work in a synodal Church.

On the question of the ordination of women, then, we would do well to reflect on Michael Dallaire's observation in *Soundings on Eucharist and Priesthood*, wherein he reminds us of the seminal role of the Holy Spirit: "The pneumatological impetus is a concept I am borrowing from Karl Rahner. Accordingly, the Spirit is not only the source of questioning but is also actively present in the development of questions, carrying them along toward answers that yield the newness of the Spirit....'What is the Spirit saying to the Church?' is the question to ask."

The ongoing task of the synod consists of being led to surprising discoveries, to have one's comforting securities displaced, and to hear anew and respond afresh to the whisperings of the Spirit.

The remaining days of the synod can be a bit destabilizing. The delegates and their advisor-experts withdraw, journalists and reporters scatter about, expectations both realistic and otherwise flourish, and we all wait for the gestation to end.

Press briefings are cancelled as the work of the drafters, refiners, and voters begin. This will take several days as they work to produce a draft of the final report: circulate among the synod members, receive amendments, incorporate them into a revised text, and then distribute it for a careful and quantified vote prior to submitting it as a complete and approved text to Pope Francis.

In the meantime, rumors flourish over what will and will not be included, politicking abounds, murmurations aplenty, embargoes everywhere, anticipations multiple and varied.

Christopher Lamb opines that there will be champagne corks

popping throughout the city in conservative quarters when the report is submitted because it will be plain for all to see that this whole synodal episode has been a catastrophic failure. Francis's dream will be shattered, the *ancien régime* secured, the flighty madness of the *synodali* over. With ecclesiastical reason back in place, Rome's authority concentrated rather than decentralized, the inflated hopes of the progressives firmly erased, and the Argentine pope once again reminded that his dangerous forays outside the accepted tradition are futile, the conservatives will rejoice that the expensive, time-consuming talk fest on the Tiber can be seen for what it was: a failed effort at substantive reform.

But that is a misreading of this Synod, although the fundamental apprehension is justified.

Synodality is not a manifesto, a creed, a platform of reformist initiatives; it is a process of ecclesial engagement. It is a maturing of a Church assembly supported by the pillars of deep listening, reverencing the other, deploying silence and prayer as tools of encounter.

If you see this as a threat to sacred governance, then you have cause to rejoice that the synod did not result in a structural or doctrinal overhaul, and you can see it as a victory for a Catholic Church unchanged by the ages.

But it would be a pyrrhic victory at the cost of an expansive collegiality and a fecund Church unity.

V

EPILOGUE

THE *FINAL REPORT*, delivered with unaccustomed alacrity and approved fully by the pontiff, is more than a hodgepodge of conciliar texts, papal addresses, and other august magisterial sources. It is a surprisingly cogent, focused, and concentrated work that provides context, detailed theological reflection—interspersed with a fair bit of ecclesiastical bafflegab and succinct summaries of the many discussion points that constituted the synod agenda.

In the report, the question of ordaining women to the diaconate remained an open one; the status of episcopal conferences and international ecclesial assemblies was affirmed and expanded; synodality was defined as generously respecting cultural diversity and the gift that is a healthy plurality.

What is most important, however, is the ringing endorsement of synodality as "a path of spiritual renewal and structured reform that enables the church to be more participatory and missionary, so that it can walk with every man and woman, radiating the life of Christ."

In other words: Global human needs are the territory to be served by a synodal strategy of Jesus-infused service. Synodality is not just for the tribe (*ad intra*) but for the world (*ad extra*).

John Henry Newman got it right—and he didn't get a mention at all. He should, for no one has explored the implications of the *sense of the faithful* more thoroughly than he.

The Synod on Synodality has now just concluded with the submission of its *Final Report* and its full and unqualified acceptance by Pope Francis as the Church's teaching on synodality.

This three-year process of discernment, consultation, assembly-gathering, and final deliberation is now over, and it was an astonishing success, but not in the way many may think.

It was not an achievement with a tally sheet of noteworthy wins: women as ordained deacons approved, LGBTQ+ requests for full incorporation into the sacramental life and rituals of the Church validated, decentralization of Church governance radically promoted.

But then, that was never really in the cards.

The success of the synod lies in Francis's embedding a process in ecclesiastical life that is constituted of a culture of encounter, a pattern of deep listening, and a reverencing of the other. This results in the uprooting of a way of being Church that has prevailed for centuries, the substitution of a top-down modus operandi et vivendi with a bottom-up percolation of missional energy and vision. It is the inverted pyramid model that Francis repeatedly invokes.

Of course, as the successor of Peter, the principle of unity in the Church, Francis is conscious of the two tensions: the centripetal pull moving toward the center and the centrifugal pull moving away from the axis. For at least two papacies—John Paul II and Benedict XVI—the centripetal was dominant; the challenge for Francis in favoring the centrifugal is to ensure that unity isn't compromised.

The *Final Report*, when speaking of national episcopal conferences and continental assemblies, strikes the right balance: "A synodal style allows local churches to move at different paces. Different paces can be valued as an expression of legitimate diversity and as an opportunity for sharing gifts and mutual enrichment."

This has been a red flag for the traditionalists—particularly as evidenced in the steady volley of firmly delivered argument by the (primarily American) traditionalist media, represented in ample numbers in the press briefings—so the appearance rather than erasure of a synodal governance model in the *Final Report* can be clocked up as a disappointment for them.

But on other fronts they must be rejoicing—Christopher Lamb's "champagne corks popping all over the city in conservative quarters celebrating the survival of the old church." Indeed, the progressive lobbies they feared would apply pressure on an unsteady pontiff to act on the call for women in ordained ministries didn't happen.

But it might be a good idea to recork.

Francis has not been defeated.

He has introduced prelates, laity, and religious to a spiritual way of being *ecclesia* that is designed to break through the boundaries of partisanship, to shatter the arrogance of the righteous, to make us all humble in the presence of the other.

Three years of preparation, reading, and synodal pedagogy have inculcated a fresh perspective on personal relations and mutual understanding in a Church context.

Although the daily press briefings—the quotidian drone fest—could often tend toward the autoreferentiality that Francis deplores, the *ad intra* preoccupations that can seduce unwary bishops actually turned out to be great boons for analysts and writers accredited by the Holy See to cover the synod.

These moments provided the coloration, the context, the passion, the angst, and the hope. Bishops from Haiti, South Sudan, the Middle East, and other war and climate-ravaged countries spoke of their anger and frustration; women religious recounted the tragic litany of abuse and clerical indifference; lay theologians provided historical context and new theological visioning.

But the challenges remain: How to implement Conversation in the Spirit methodology throughout the universal Church? How to ensure the structural support for institutional change?

Nathalie Becquart, a sister of the Congregation of Xavières, is one of the two undersecretaries of the General Secretariat of the Synod and indispensable to the effective running of the synod. She spoke to me of the implementation of synodality in the many African and Asian jurisdictions she has visited between the two sessions of the synod. The implementation, the momentum, and the architecture of these multiple and diverse experiments in synodality are essentially lay-propelled and enacted.

And this brings us back to Newman.

In his 1859 work, *On Consulting the Faithful in Matters of Doctrine*, the future English cardinal made it clear that there were four specific historical moments when the laity "saved" the Church. The enfleshment of synodality may well be the next iteration.

Given Francis's inverted pyramid model, synodality is a gift the laity can run with, strengthening the common baptism of all believers, driving a new era of co-responsibility and accountability. The arguments for excluding women have never been compelling, and now the *synodali* are guaranteeing its durability as a recurring topic. It won't go away because it can't go away. As a synodal Church emerges out of a local dynamic propelled by a committed Catholic laity, the encrustations of clericalism will crumble.

Francis is not an innovator pope: no new doctrines, no sundering departures from past practices. But he is a disruptor pope: he has disrupted established patterns of past synods, modifying their structure and expanding their purpose. He has disrupted expectations of papal involvement. He has freed the synod to be constructively creative rather than supine and cautious.

In keeping with his plan to bring the teachings of the Second Vatican Council fully into the life of the Church, the *Final Report* underlines the progress made thus far: "The synodal journey constitutes an authentic further act of reception of the Council, thus deepening its inspiration and reinvigorating its prophetic force for today's world."

The success then of the Synod on Synodality lies not in its summary document nor papal approbation. It lies in its pastoral strategy: "giving us the 'spiritual taste' of what it means to be the People of God."

The laity empowered; Newman vindicated.

The early months of 2025 saw Francis struggling with several severe physical ailments; he was hospitalized for an extended period of time; his doctors feared for his life; he achieved some kind of equilibrium and under strict instructions to reduce his workload was allowed to return to his home in the Casa Santa Marta. He appeared to be slowly improving but on Easter Sunday, April 20, he delivered what was to be his last Easter Blessing to the City of Rome and the World, his *Ubi et Orbi*, and what was to prove his last trip by popemobile around the Piazza di San Pietro. He ate his evening meal, retired to bed, and in the early hours of Easter Monday, April 22, he died from a stroke and heart attack.

On March 11, Francis—as outlined in Cardinal Mario Grech's "Letter on the Accompaniment Process of the Implementation Phase of the Synod"—approved "the start of a process of accompaniment and evaluation of the implementation phase by the General Secretariat of the Synod" as he wanted to ensure that "synodality is increasingly understood and lived as an essential dimension of the ordinary life of local Churches and the entire Church."

In other words, synodality is not going away.

Francis's death provided the world with an opportunity to assess his many accomplishments, to think again about the arresting originality of a Jesuit who humanized the papacy. As

Canadian Prime Minister Mark Carney observed on the day of the pontiff's death: "Francis was the moral conscience of the world."

It's all in the name. When Jorge Mario Bergoglio was elected pope on March 13, 2013, he chose to be known as Francis.

The first of many firsts that have come to define the Bergoglio papacy, he knew that by choosing a name foreign to the annals of papal appellations he was breaking with convention, just as Albino Luciani had done when he chose the double-barreled John Paul I.

He knew he needed to explain why he had chosen Francis—and did so at a large gathering of journalists three days after the conclave that elected him. It turned out to be a profound moment, demonstrating his own comfort level with the media, his preference for transparency over speculation, and his resolve to embrace the legacy, not only the name, of St. Francis, *Il Poverello*, the Poor One of Assisi.

"For me, he is the man of poverty, the man of peace, the man who protects creation," he said. "How I would like a church which is poor and for the poor."

Creating a Church of and for the poor proved a titanic task for Francis. Bishops and cardinals accustomed to fine living, sumptuous housing, and the perks and privileges ratified by centuries of convention were stunned to discover that the newly elected pope from Argentina preferred a stripped-down papacy—not the Apostolic Palace, the official residence of popes, but the comparatively simple digs of the Casa Santa Marta. Protocol was streamlined. The princely dignities of office much modified.

By taking the name of Francis, Bergoglio signaled his intention to direct the Church in new ways and to do so from the very beginning of his Petrine ministry.

As the first pope from the Jesuit order, he elected to make his inaugural papal visit to Lampedusa, an island off the southwest coast of Italy, to visit migrants from North Africa who had braved rough, sometimes deadly seas to escape tyranny, war, and poverty. These were the ones he was called to serve, and this too was a first.

The two previous popes, on their premiere trips outside the Vatican, had gone to their homelands—Poland and Germany, respectively. But Francis, to the dismay of his officials, opted for Lampedusa and, in doing so, sent a message to the world.

This trip wasn't a photo op, a media ploy, a dramatic papal visit to a territory distant from Vatican concerns. On the contrary, the gesture was a visually arresting pilgrimage to the peripheries—and therefore a key component of the Francis agenda.

Throughout his papacy, Francis repeatedly underscored the role of the margins—geographical, political, economic, cultural, and theological. For too long, those on the edges had been made to feel either alienated or of secondary concern. No longer. The peripheries became the focal point of the pope's priorities.

From the outset, many in the Vatican's head office—the Roman curia—sensed that their new boss was not going to follow established ways; that he would opt for spontaneity over script, shuffle things around—make (as he urged Catholic youth to do) a mess.

When I asked Bergoglio's old friend Rabbi Abraham Skorka, a fellow Argentine, scientist, and the leading Jewish figure in the pope's home country, about the growing perception in conservative Catholic circles that Francis was out of his depth in the Vatican, that he would be sidelined by the curia, that his ambitions for change would be squandered by internal disputes, and that he would be dismissed as a lightweight by the old guard keen on securing a deferential continuity with the John Paul II and Benedict XVI papacies, the rabbi thundered: "They don't know my Jorge."

But they came to know Jorge very quickly. When Benedict XVI resigned, it was clear to the cardinal electors that his successor would need to rein in a curia that was out of control, handle the spiraling morale issue around the many scandals—venal and venereal—swirling about the Vatican's many offices, and deal with a Catholic hierarchy unhappy with decades of centralized management.

No easy feat, but Bergoglio's candidacy provided a light at the end of the tunnel. He was not implicated in any Vatican dysfunction, was unfamiliar with the Roman manner of doing things, and was disinclined by temperament to adjust to it. He was a fresh face and would unsettle the status quo.

What most of the electors would not have known—with the exception of his Latin American confreres—was his tenacity, disciplined focus, and radical pastoral style.

He would clean house, and the scouring would be much more comprehensive than most would have expected.

He established the Council of Cardinals, drawn from global constituencies that could provide him with broad and frank advice. He began to make serious inroads from the outset in getting the Church's financial house in order and appointed the steely, competent, and ruthlessly conservative Cardinal George Pell of Australia to head the new Secretariat for the Economy in 2014.

Francis didn't flinch from dismissing obscurantist prelates who were either underperforming or corrupt, including the powerful Cardinal Giovanni Angelo Becciu (then-Prefect of the Dicastery for the Causes of Saints) on grounds of alleged embezzlement.

The new pope fired laity who failed to ensure fiscal probity and instituted a ceiling for pensions for cardinals. He even railed against some Church officials' penchant for spacious living quarters and perks.

Purging the financial skullduggery embedded in centuries of consolidated power occupied Francis for his entire papacy. But it wasn't just the financial quagmire of the Vatican that he addressed—it was also the need to restructure the entire governance operation.

For the first nine years of his papacy, Francis worked to reconceive the curial bureaucracy to make it genuinely catholic—meaning universal—and after massive consultation with the entire hierarchy, he issued his precedent-setting reforms with the publication of *Praedicate Evangelium* in 2022.

The central highlight of this document is its assertion that mission and professional accountability are not tied to ordination. Therefore, officeholders in the Church's governance structure need not be clerics, they could be competent laypeople.

If Francis's achievements were limited to internal reform and management priorities, his pontificate would have fallen far short of his vision for a missionary, outward-looking, and gospel-centered ministry.

Francis articulated his ecclesial vision with his first apostolic exhortation, *Evangelii Gaudium*, at the very beginning of his pontificate. It was his charter document (or strategic plan) and vividly underlined his commitment to serving everyone in the spirit of the gospel. None were to be excluded.

His clear preference was for a "church that is bruised, hurting, and dirty because it has been out on the streets" over "a church that is sick from being confined and clinging to its own security."

Throughout his papacy, he insisted on clergy having the "smell of the sheep." He wanted priests and bishops to have the well-being of their congregants as their primary obligation, to eschew the comforts of their clerical status and to view social justice not as a decorative ornament of their priesthood but as constitutive of their life of service.

To that end, he encouraged his nuncios, or papal ambassadors, to only promote future bishops after a careful discernment of their pastoral sensitivity. He cautioned seminary rectors against recruiting and forming candidates who were enamored of clerical dress or who harbored dangerous nostalgia for the trappings of the old Church.

He admonished prelates who did not live according to the standards of the gospel but rather as princelings disconnected from the people they are obligated to serve. As one can imagine, he made many enemies of those who had invested much in their ecclesiastical careers and who saw in his remaking of priestly life a diminution of their own status.

But Francis was not deterred. In fact, as his papacy unfolded, he became bolder and bolder. He berated his own staff at the annual Christmas oration to the curia (for what he felt was cliquey workplace behavior) and increasingly addressed the larger world across the Tiber River.

In *Laudato Si'*, his encyclical on the environment as our common home, with its promotion of an "integral ecology," Francis called the world to action, setting out a blueprint for an ecological recovery that crossed all ideological, political, and religious boundaries. While his views bolstered his standing in circles outside Catholicism, it also served as a *tuba mirum* (an alarm bell of sorts) for conservative Catholics, specifically in the moneyed classes, who saw yet again the pope's disdain for the orthodox economics that defined Western success.

Despite growing opposition, most significantly from powerful U.S. sectors of the Church, Francis persisted in seeking a human unity that transcended special interests, imperialist ambitions, and technological mastery.

He knew that authentic peace among countries could only be realized when there was peace among religions; that dialogue and cooperation grounded in the real and not in abstractions demanded contact.

To that end, he traveled to remote regions of the world, to war zones, and to places that would not ordinarily welcome the Bishop of Rome. More than any previous pontiff, he built solid relations with Islam, including the epoch-making 2019 *Document on Human Fraternity for World Peace and Living Together*, co-authored with Sheik Ahmadal-Tayyeb, Grand Imam of the al-Azhar Mosque and University in Egypt.

The success Francis garnered with his various forays into the larger world outside the Catholic orbit—although at 1.4 billion members, it is not an insignificant constituency—was not always welcomed in traditionalist Catholic communities.

His relaxation of the rules for divorced and remarried Catholics regarding their access to the Eucharist, allowing for greater pastoral discretion at the local episcopal level; his refusal to judge gay Catholics and his warm embrace of various leaders of the LGBTQ community; and his enthusiastic promotion of women in the Vatican, unparalleled in number and prominence, infuriated many Catholics, confounded some bishops, and hardened the opposition he faced internally.

Catholic author Paul Elie identified the danger in Francis's incrementalism—his slow and careful nuancing of Catholic teachings, which saw ambiguity replace rock-hard clarity during his tenure.

Ironically, Francis's strenuous efforts to address intractable global problems served to draw attention away from the problem near at hand—namely, that when it comes to sexuality, "the church's account of the human person is as superannuated as trickle-down economics and coal-burning power plants," he wrote.

Finding a spiritual and moral equipoise was a constant during Francis's ministry as the Successor of Peter—holding the sacred deposit of doctrine in balance with the challenges associated with a new anthropology. He refused to be held enthralled to evanescent ideological trends even as he refused to be held captive on a procrustean bed of unalterable truths.

Francis fought with some success to contend with the clerical sex-abuse scandals but faltered on several occasions by misreading the signs on the ground. His steadfast support for a Chilean bishop implicated in a cover-up, and of a priest whose notoriety as an abuser profoundly damaged the moral authority of the Chilean hierarchy, threatened to scuttle his own moral stature.

Once apprised of all the details, he relented, apologized, and changed course. Still, the incident sent a message to many sexual-abuse survivors that Francis didn't quite grasp the enormity of the problem.

But with his direct intervention in the case of the Comboni Fathers and their record of abuse at a school in West Yorkshire, England, in 2023 (he met with many of the survivors personally and interceded on their behalf), he provided hard proof that he had indeed come to understand the enormity of the damage.

Similarly, with the agonized calls for justice by Indigenous peoples and a recognition of their suffering at the hands of a Church that was often complicit in colonial oppression, Pope Francis rose to the occasion in Bolivia and in Canada, sometimes with only tepid support from local religious authorities.

The Bergoglio papacy opted for mercy over doctrine, inclusion over exclusion, moral resilience over legal certitude, and the priority of intuition over certainty. Faith over fear.

In the end, for the duration of his decade-plus pontificate, Francis was the disruptor pope: disrupting the established pattern of doing things by replacing a magisterial with a synodal way of being a Church, with less hierarchy and more lay involvement; disrupting the spiritual and intellectual complacency that besets institutional Catholicism; disrupting an ahistorical understanding of the Church that shields us from the reforming gusts of the Spirit.

His papal style reshaped the papacy. Permanently.

VI

POSTLUDE

Habemus Papam

THE CARDINAL PROTODEACON, Dominique Memberti, intoned
from the central loggia the well-worn words in Latin that
proclaim to the world the new Bishop of Rome: *Annuntio vobis
gaudium magnum: Habemus papam!* (I announce to you a great
joy: We have a pope!)

Not only a new pope, but a surprising one. Robert Francis
Prevost—the prefect of the Dicastery of Bishops, president of the
Pontifical Commission for Latin America, and for over a dozen years
prior general of the Order of St. Augustine, the Augustinians—
was chosen by his fellow cardinal electors to become the Supreme
Pontiff, Successor of St. Peter, and Head of the Vatican City State,
among other titles, dignities, and responsibilities.

He is a surprising choice because although his name surfaced in some of the lists of *papabili*, or those considered likely
candidates for the papacy, he was not ranked in the first tier.
But he has been around for some time doing the kinds of things
that position you nicely for the highest leadership in the Roman

Catholic Church: pastoral work, missionary experience, gaining comprehensive language skills, managing oversight of a religious order with extensive global reach, earning a canon law doctorate from a Roman pontifical university, and amassing senior Vatican governance exposure.

He is a surprising choice as well in that he is an American, and the College of Cardinals has been hitherto wary about electing a citizen of the United States to the Petrine Office. That wariness, in part, stems from Rome's condemnation of the heresy of Americanism—as it was called by no less a figure than Leo XIII. This "heresy" consisted in ways of thinking that attempted to align American political values and their cultural ethos with traditional Roman Catholic tenets and historical practices. In other words, Rome looked askance at various developments in the new world that put at peril the integrity of the Catholic tradition. It didn't help that the new world was a predominantly Protestant, and in some cases virulently anti-Catholic, society.

Rome's anti-Americanist sympathies persisted for decades before being laid to rest because of the Second Vatican Council (1962–1965), the rapid increase in the U.S. Catholic population because of mass immigration from Catholic countries in Europe, and the rise of confidence in the American Catholic Church as a major player in the political life of the country.

One thing Leo XIV has done is put a stake in the heart of Leo XIII's anxiety over American Catholic fidelity to the Holy See. A son of Chicago now calls the shots in the Vatican.

Born to a French father and an Italian mother, Prevost earned a bachelor of science degree in mathematics from the Augustinian Villanova University in Philadelphia in 1977—the same year that he joined the Augustinians. He was ordained a priest of that order in 1982 and shortly after began a long association with Peru, serving as chancellor of the Territorial Prelature of Chulucanas, and eventually heading the Augustinian seminary in Trujillo.

Although he would return to the States to serve as a provincial of his order in 1999, and then shortly—in 2001—be elected as the head of the entire order, he would return to Peru as bishop of Chiclayo in 2015. He took on additional episcopal responsibilities in the country before being called to Rome in January 2023 to serve as the head of the bishop-making department in the curial bureaucracy (a very critical and key position in the Vatican hierarchy), and in September of the same year he was created a cardinal by Pope Francis.

Certainly Francis was impressed by Prevost's missionary credentials, his easy command of Spanish, his support for the Argentine pope's synodality undertaking—a reshaping of the Church in keeping with the teachings of the Second Vatican Council—and his generally irenic personality.

By choosing to take the name Leo—given that Leo XIII was also the pope who ushered in over a century of Catholic social teaching with his 1891 encyclical *Rerum Novarum*—Prevost has sent a clear message of papal continuity. He also adroitly avoided feeding the toxicity amongst various Catholic factions by not opting for Benedict XVII or Francis II—and by stretching back over a century to the first modern pope, he confirmed his allegiance to Catholic social doctrine without whipping up hostilities between the Bergoglio and Ratzinger camps.

Leo XIII is better known for his revival and endorsement of the philosophical and theological thought of St. Thomas Aquinas—and his championing of laborers and their rights in industrial Europe—than he is for his condemnation of Americanism, so Prevost's election is a sweet vindication of the pastoral fecundity and ardor of American Catholics.

It is also more than that. By choosing an American with international exposure, a refined social justice sensitivity, and a commitment to the priorities of Francis regarding socioeconomic inequity, global migration, and the evils of ethno-nationalism, the cardinals have set up on the Tiber an antidote to the insularity and intolerance on the Potomac. A true bridge builder, or *pontifex maximus*.

But I suspect that there is a more conservative streak in Leo XIV than Francis. The fact that he chose to wear the traditional papal regalia when he first appeared on the balcony, in sharp contrast with Francis's eschewing the elaborate apostolic stole, is more than a fashion statement. He likely will be more conventionally papal in his behavior.

That said, as I have indicated Leo's support for synodality is unwavering. His attendance at both sessions of the synod was marked by his earnest engagement. He also highlighted in his initial *Urbi et Orbi* blessing from the apostolic loggia, when greeting the thousands below in the Piazza di San Pietro on the day of his election: "To all of you, brothers and sisters of Rome, of Italy, of the whole world, we want to be a synodal church, a church that walks, that always seeks peace, that always seeks charity, that always seeks to be close especially to those who suffer."

He also confessed that as a "son of Saint Augustine, who said: 'With you I am a Christian and for you a bishop,'" he has underlined his pledge to function as a synodal Bishop of Rome.

The synodal journey continues.

NOTES

I. PRELUDE

1. Alexandra Schwartz, "Memory Serves: How Annie Ernaux Turns the Past into Art," *New Yorker*, November 21, 2022, 17.

2. Anne Chisholm, "The Flight of the Mind," review of *The Diary of Virginia Woolf*, vol. 1–5, *The Tablet*, July 29, 2023, 17.

3. John O'Malley, "The Hermeneutic of Reform: An Historical Analysis," *Theological Studies* 73, no. 3 (September 2012): 540.

4. T. Howland Sanks, SJ. "Episcopal Collegiality and Synodality: Seeking a New 'Social Imaginary,'" *La Civiltà Cattolica*, August 16, 2023.

5. Anthony Tonnos, "Definitions and Directions," *Grail: An Ecumenical Journal* (March 1986): 72.

6. Dominique Le Tourneau, "Synod of Bishops," in *The Papacy: An Encyclopedia*, ed. Philippe Levillain, vol. 3 (London: Routledge, 2002), 1478.

7. Paul Vallely, *Pope Francis: Untying the Knots* (London: Bloomsbury, 2013), 184–85.

8. Michael Czerny, SJ, "Towards a Synodal Church," *La Civiltà Cattolica*, January 25, 2021.

9. Austen Ivereigh, *Wounded Shepherd: Pope Francis and His Struggle to Convert the Catholic Church* (New York: Holt, 2019), 89.

10. John Henry Newman, *On Consulting the Faithful in Matters of Doctrine*, ed. John Coulson (London: Collins, 1986), 106.

11. John Henry Newman, *Apologia pro Vita Sua*, ed. Martin J. Svaglic (Oxford: Oxford University Press, 1967), 226.

12. Joseph W. Tobin, "The Long Game: Pope Francis's Vision of Synodality," *Commonweal* (June 2021): 26.

13. Cardinal Shönborn, interview by François Vayne, *Jerusalem Cross* (2021–2022), 3–4.

14. Daniel E. Flores, "Closeness and the Common Journey: Synodality as an Expression of the Church's Responsiveness to Christ," *Commonweal* (June 2022): 31.

15. Catherine E. Clifford, *Go, Rebuild My House*, ecclesial reform blog posted on the website of Sacred Heart University, Fairfield, CT.

16. North American Working Group, *Doing Theology from the Existential Peripheries Report*, 9.

17. Archbishop Don Bolen, interview by Michael Higgins, September 27, 2023.

II. THE FIRST SESSION

1. Christopher Lamb, interview by Michael Higgins, October 9, 2023.

2. Christopher White, interview by Michael Higgins, October 12, 2023.

3. October 9, 2021.

III. THE INTERREGNUM

1. Giacomo Costa, SJ, "Toward the Second Session of the 2021–2024 Synod," *La Civiltà Cattolica*, May 24, 2024, 5.

REFERENCES

Chisholm, Anne. Review of *The Diary of Virginia Woolf*, volumes 1–5. *The Tablet*, July 29, 2023.

Clifford, Catherine E. *Go, Rebuild My House*. Ecclesial reform blog posted on the website of Sacred Heart University, Fairfield, CT.

Costa, Giacoma, SJ. "Toward the Second Session of the 2021–2024 Synod." *La Civiltà Cattolica*, May 24, 2024.

Czerny, Michael, SJ. "Towards a Synodal Church." *La Civiltà Cattolica*, January 25, 2021.

Flores, Daniel E. "Closeness and the Common Journey: Synodality as an Expression of the Church's Responsiveness to Christ." *Commonweal* (June 2022).

Higgins, Michael W. *The Church Needs the Laity: The Wisdom of John Henry Newman*. Mahwah, NJ: Paulist Press, 2021.

———. "Greene's Priest: A Sort of Rebel." In *Essays in Graham Greene: An Annual Review*, vol. 3., edited by Peter Wolfe. St. Louis: Lucas Hall Press, 1992.

———. Interview with Archbishop Don Bolen in the Office of the President of St. Jerome's University, Waterloo, Ontario, on September 27, 2023, following Archbishop Bolen's public address at the St. Jerome's Centre Catholic Experience Lectures: "The Wounds of the Past, Truth-Telling and a Future of Hope: The Doctrine of Discovery and the Path of Reconciliation."

———. Interview with Christopher Lamb, October 9, 2023, Rome.

———. Interview with Christopher White, October 12, 2023, Rome.

Ivereigh, Austen. *Wounded Shepherd: Pope Francis and His Struggle to Convert the Catholic Church.* New York: Holt, 2019.

Le Tourneau, Dominique, "Synod of Bishops." In *The Papacy: An Encyclopedia.* Vol. 3. Edited by Philippe Levillain. London: Routledge, 2002.

Newman, John Henry. *Apologia pro Vita Sua.* Edited by Martin J. Svaglic. Oxford: Oxford University Press, 1967.

———. *On Consulting the Faithful in Matters of Doctrine.* Edited by John Coulson. London: Collins, 1986.

O'Malley, John. "The Hermeneutic of Reform: An Historical Analysis." *Theological Studies* 73, no. 3 (September 2012): 517–46.

Sanks, T. Howland, SJ. "Episcopal Collegiality and Synodality: Seeking a New 'Social Imaginary.'" *La Civiltà Cattolica*, August 16, 2023.

Schwartz, Alexandra. "Memory Serves: How Annie Ernaux Turns the Past into Art." *The New Yorker*, November 21, 2022.

Tobin, Joseph W. "The Long Game: Pope Francis's Vision of Synodality." *Commonweal* (June 2021).

Tonnos, Anthony. "Definitions and Directions." *Grail: An Ecumenical Journal* (March 1986).

Vallely, Paul. *Pope Francis: Untying the Knots.* London: Bloomsbury, 2013.

Vayne, François. Interview with Cardinal Shönborn. *Jerusalem Cross* (2021–2022): 3–4.